A Freshman's Guide to Criminal Justice

Pathways to Success

by

Gary D. Will Jr.

innovativeink
PUBLISHING
A Division of Kendall Hunt

Cover courtesy Gary Will

innovativeink
PUBLISHING

www.innovativeinkpublishing.com
Send all inquiries to:
4050 Westmark Drive
Dubuque, IA 52004-1840

Print ISBN: 979-8-3851-4428-0
Ebook ISBN: 979-8-3851-4429-7

Published in the United States of America

This book is dedicated to my students

Contents

Introduction

Welcome to the intricate and compelling world of criminal justice studies. As you embark on this educational journey, you're not merely choosing a discipline; you're stepping into a realm that sits at the confluence of law, ethics, and society. This book is crafted to serve as your compass, guiding you through the complexities of the criminal justice system and equipping you with the knowledge and skills needed to navigate your college experience successfully.

Studying criminal justice is an adventure that will challenge your perceptions and expand your intellectual horizons. The field is as diverse as it is dynamic, covering areas from policing, legal processes, and corrections to the broader societal issues that underpin criminal behavior and law enforcement. You'll learn not only about the mechanics of the criminal justice system but also about the profound implications of justice and how it affects real lives.

Success in criminal justice studies requires more than just passion and determination. It demands a unique set of academic and interpersonal skills, an understanding of complex and often contentious issues, and the ability to apply theoretical knowledge to real-world problems. This book aims to lay a solid foundation for these skills, offering insights into the most effective study habits, tips for engaging with your courses, and strategies for leveraging university resources.

One of the first steps to mastering the discipline is understanding its interdisciplinary nature. Criminal justice draws upon psychology, sociology, political science, and law, demanding a broad yet nuanced approach to learning. We'll delve into the major components of the criminal justice system—law enforcement, court systems, and corrections—while emphasizing the importance of viewing these elements within a larger societal context.

As you navigate your first year, developing essential study habits and time management skills will be crucial. Engaging deeply with your courses will allow you to absorb the rich content and develop a critical perspective that is indispensable in criminal justice studies. We'll provide practical advice on how to make the most of your education from day one.

General education courses might seem unrelated to your major, but they are vital in broadening your understanding and developing a well-rounded perspective. These courses complement your major studies, equipping you with the analytical and communication skills essential for success in the criminal justice field.

Leveraging university resources is another key theme of this book. From the library and online databases to the writing center and tutoring services, making use of these resources can enhance your academic performance and support your research efforts. Furthermore, mastering APA formatting is critical for criminal justice majors, as it is the standard for writing and citing sources in the discipline. We'll guide you through the basics of APA style, ensuring your academic work meets the highest standards.

Crafting excellent academic work is a central part of your studies. This involves understanding your assignments, developing effective research and note-taking strategies, and learning how to craft and revise your arguments. Beyond the classroom, we'll explore the value of experiential learning through internships, volunteer opportunities, and networking, which can provide invaluable real-world experience and professional connections.

Technology also plays a crucial role in criminal justice studies. We'll introduce you to essential software and tools, helping you develop the digital literacy skills needed for research, presentations, and future professional endeavors. As you prepare for advanced courses, understanding key themes, theories, and the importance of foundational knowledge will be essential for deepening your expertise in the field.

Looking toward the future, we'll discuss planning your academic path, exploring career options within the criminal justice field, and considering graduate studies. Professional skills such as communication, ethical decision-making, and leadership are also vital, and this book will offer tips and strategies for developing these competencies.

Finally, we'll take a global perspective, comparing international criminal justice systems and examining the impact of globalization. This will highlight the diverse approaches to justice around the world and the importance of understanding criminal justice in a global context.

This book is more than just a guide; it's a companion on your journey through the world of criminal justice studies. It's designed to inspire, motivate, and equip you with the knowledge and skills necessary to thrive in this field. As you turn each page, remember that you're not just studying a discipline; you're preparing to make a meaningful impact on society.

In the chapters that follow, we will navigate the depths of the criminal justice system, explore strategies for academic success, and lay the groundwork for a fulfilling career in the field. The journey ahead is both challenging and rewarding, and it promises to transform not only your understanding of criminal justice but also your role in creating a more just society.

Welcome to the beginning of an incredible adventure in learning and discovery. Let's embark on this journey together, with curiosity, courage, and a relentless pursuit of justice.

Chapter 1: Decoding the Criminal Justice System

Embarking on the journey to decode the criminal justice system offers an enlightening pathway to understanding the intricate fabric that holds our society together. This chapter serves as your initial foray into a complex world where law enforcement, the courts, and the corrections system operate both independently and interdependently to maintain order, ensure justice, and promote rehabilitation. At its core, the criminal justice system is a multifaceted entity, characterized by a diversity of roles, responsibilities, and challenges that span the societal spectrum. By dissecting its major components, students can appreciate the depth and breadth of the field they are about to immerse themselves in. The significance of adopting an interdisciplinary approach cannot be overstated, as it encourages critical thinking and offers a holistic perspective on the justice system's operation and its impact on society (Clear, Reisig, & Cole, 2020). Engaging with this discipline requires a commitment to understanding its complexity and recognizing the importance of each component in the broader justice framework. Through this exploration, you'll be equipped not just with knowledge but with a profound respect for the delicate balance between upholding the law and preserving human rights. This chapter lays the foundation for a rewarding academic and professional journey, highlighting the vital need for dedicated, ethical, and knowledgeable individuals in the criminal justice field.

Understanding the Major Components

In embarking on the intricate study of the criminal justice system, it's crucial for students, especially freshmen entering the college arena, to grasp the foundational structures that uphold this vast field. At its core, the criminal justice system is segmented into three pivotal components: law enforcement, the court systems, and corrections. Each sector plays a specific, yet interconnected role in the administration of justice, starting from law enforcement agencies that initiate the process by upholding laws and apprehending offenders, moving through the court systems where the legality of actions is dissected, and culminating with corrections which implement the sentences and strive for rehabilitation (Cole, Smith, & DeJong, 2019). Understanding these components offers a compass for navigating the broader system's complexities, illuminating the path for those who are poised to reform, advocate, or interpret the law. As emphasized by academia, a firm comprehension of these components not only enhances scholarly pursuit but serves to inspire innovative solutions to age-old judicial issues (Walker & Katz, 2018). Through this exploration, students are encouraged to envision their roles within this mosaic, poised to make impactful contributions to justice and society at large (Clear, Reisig, & Cole, 2020).

Law Enforcement In the expanse of the criminal justice system, law enforcement acts as the frontline, embodying both the shield and the spear in society's perennial quest for harmony and order. As freshmen embarking on the study of the criminal justice system, understanding the multifaceted nature of law enforcement is not only essential but transformative. This exploration travels through the veins of history, theory, policy, and the unyielding human spirit that animates the badge.

At the onset, it's pivotal to grasp the broad spectrum of roles that law enforcement officers embody. These roles stretch beyond the traditional patrol duties to encompass community engagement, investigative work, and increasingly, the navigation of complex technological landscapes. The scientific advancements in forensic science, digital investigations, and crime scene analysis have revolutionized how law enforcement agencies operate, a testament to the field's dynamic evolution.

Despite the technological strides, the heart of law enforcement remains its people. The daily reality for officers includes not only confronting crime but also addressing social issues such as homelessness, mental illness, and substance abuse. Here, the intersection of law enforcement with social services is paramount, revealing the need for officers to be as adept in empathy and communication as they are in tactical skills. This dual capacity underscores the importance of a well-rounded education in the criminal justice arena.

Engagement with the community stands as a cornerstone of effective law enforcement. Community policing strategies, which emphasize building relationships and working collaboratively with the communities served, have been shown to significantly improve public safety outcomes (Jones & Smith, 2019). Such strategies demonstrate the shift from a solely reactive force to a proactive partner in community well-being.

The legal framework governing law enforcement operations is both deep and wide. Understanding the constitutional rights guaranteed to citizens, including the Fourth Amendment's protections against unreasonable searches and seizures, and the Sixth Amendment's right to counsel, is crucial for aspiring law enforcement professionals. These legal underpinnings not only guide the actions of officers but also protect the integrity of the criminal justice process and the rights of all individuals involved.

Accountability in law enforcement has never been more scrutinized. The advent of body-worn cameras and the proliferation of digital media has brought law enforcement actions into the public eye with unprecedented immediacy. This transparency, while challenging, offers an unparalleled opportunity for law enforcement agencies to build trust within the communities they serve.

Further, the role of leadership within law enforcement agencies cannot be overstated. The ethos of an agency, shaped by its leaders, influences every aspect of its operations, from day-to-day interactions with the public to critical incident responses. Leadership in law enforcement is not merely a position but a practice that embeds values of integrity, accountability, and service into the fabric of the organization.

The psychological and emotional demands placed on law enforcement officers are profound. The exposure to traumatic events, the stress of life-and-death decisions, and the weight of public expectation can take a toll. Criminal justice students need to recognize the importance of mental health resources and resilience strategies for those in the field.

Education plays a pivotal role in preparing new entrants to the law enforcement field. Progressive criminal justice programs now offer a blend of theory, practical skills, and experiential learning to equip students with a holistic view of the field. This educational paradigm ensures that graduates not only understand the historical and legal frameworks but are also adept in the latest technological and social skills required in modern law enforcement.

For those studying criminal justice, the exploration of law enforcement offers a unique lens through which to view the complexities of human behavior, societal norms, and legal principles. It is a study that challenges the mind, stirs the heart, and calls forth a commitment to service grounded in justice and compassion.

As emerging scholars and practitioners in the field of criminal justice, students are encouraged to approach the study of law enforcement with curiosity, an open mind, and a commitment to ethical reflection. The path is rigorous, filled with both challenges and opportunities, yet it is through this journey that the next generation of law enforcement professionals will emerge, ready to contribute to the evolution of a just and safe society.

The interplay between law enforcement and the communities served is an ongoing dialogue, one that requires continuous engagement, evaluation, and adaptation. As criminal justice students delve into this dynamic field, they embark on a journey of learning that extends far beyond the classroom, into the very heart of society itself.

In conclusion, law enforcement, as a fundamental component of the criminal justice system, offers an array of challenges and opportunities for those dedicated to upholding justice. The journey through its complexities is not just an academic pursuit but a calling that demands integrity, courage, and a deep-seated commitment to public service. The study of law enforcement in the context of criminal justice education is not merely preparatory; it is transformative, equipping tomorrow's leaders with the knowledge, skills, and moral compass to navigate the challenges of an ever-evolving societal landscape.

Court Systems

In the weave of the criminal justice fabric, the court system stands as the intermediary framework where laws are interpreted, and justice is meted out. This intricate dance between law and liberty is pivotal for freshmen embarking on a journey through the criminal justice system. Understanding its nuances not only aids in academic success but also lights the path toward a promising career.

The American court system is bifurcated into federal and state jurisdictions, a design that mirrors the complexity and diversity of the nation itself. Spanning across this spectrum are courts of limited jurisdiction, general jurisdiction, appellate courts, and the ultimate arbiter of legal disputes, the United States Supreme Court. Each of these layers plays a distinct role in the judicial process, and grasping these roles is the first step in demystifying the legal system.

At the foundation are the courts of limited jurisdiction, often referred to as lower courts. These courts handle specific types of cases, such as traffic violations, small claims, and preliminary hearings in criminal cases. An understanding of their function provides insight into how the majority of legal disputes and initial stages of criminal cases are processed.

Moving up the hierarchy, courts of general jurisdiction—commonly known as trial courts—handle a broader spectrum of cases, including serious criminal offenses, civil cases, and family law. These courts are where facts are established, and the law is applied to individual cases—a fundamental concept that underlines the court's role in the justice system.

The appellate courts serve a different purpose. Instead of determining the facts of a case, these courts review how the law was applied in trial courts. They ensure the law is interpreted consistently and justice is administered fairly across the board. The ability to analyze appellate court opinions is a critical skill for students, offering deep insights into legal reasoning and judicial processes.

At the pinnacle of the court hierarchy stands the United States Supreme Court. Its decisions not only resolve specific legal disputes but also shape the course of American law and society. The Supreme Court's rulings serve as precedents, guiding lower courts in the interpretation and application of the law. Engaging with these landmark cases cultivates a deeper understanding of constitutional principles and their real-world implications.

Understanding the distinctive roles and responsibilities of each court within the system underscores the complexity and sophistication of legal adjudication. It's this foundational knowledge that enables students to critically analyze legal issues and fosters an appreciation for the dynamic interplay between law and society.

The procedural aspects of the court system, including the stages of a criminal trial, plea bargaining, and the appeals process, are vital components of the judicial landscape.

Mastery of these procedures not only enriches students' academic capabilities but also prepares them for real-world application in internships and future careers.

Jurisdiction, the authority of a court to hear a case, is a central concept that necessitates thorough comprehension. The distinction between original jurisdiction and appellate jurisdiction, along with an understanding of subject matter jurisdiction and personal jurisdiction, are fundamental in navigating the legal environment effectively.

The adversarial system, a hallmark of the American legal process, pits opposing sides against each other in pursuit of the truth. This competitive framework is predicated on the belief that truth arises from the vigorous contest of ideas—a notion that underpins critical thinking and analytical skills essential for criminal justice students.

Another facet of the court system that demands attention is the role of the legal professionals within it. Judges, prosecutors, defense attorneys, and other courtroom personnel work in concert to ensure the wheels of justice turn smoothly. An appreciation for the duties and ethical obligations of these legal actors enriches one's understanding of the system's integrity and function.

Moreover, the impact of technology on the court system is a burgeoning area of interest. Digital innovations are transforming court proceedings, from electronic filing of documents to virtual courtrooms. Awareness of these technological advancements is crucial for students preparing to enter a legal landscape that is increasingly dependent on digital tools.

The court system, with its hierarchy of structures and complex procedures, may seem daunting at first glance. However, its exploration is both a challenge and an opportunity. It provides a venue for critical thinking, problem-solving, and the application of legal principles in practical scenarios—skills that are invaluable in the pursuit of a criminal justice degree.

Embracing the study of court systems with curiosity and diligence, therefore, is not merely an academic exercise. It is a journey toward becoming a knowledgeable, ethical, and effective participant in the criminal justice arena. For those who embark on this path, the rewards are profound, both personally and professionally.

The study of court systems is, in essence, a study of the balance between order and freedom, between society's need for security and the individual's right to justice. It's a dynamic field that constantly evolves with societal changes and legal innovations. As criminal justice students delve into this fascinating area, they lay the groundwork for promising careers dedicated to the service of justice and the betterment of society.

Corrections and Rehabilitation Within the broad spectrum of the criminal justice system, the corrections component stands as a testament to the dual principles of punishment and rehabilitation. Its Undeniable complexity and the sheer scale of the correctional system in the United States demand a nuanced understanding, especially for those embarking on a journey through criminal justice studies. This section aims to dissect the multifaceted nature of corrections, highlighting its evolution, challenges, and the pivotal role it plays in societal protection and offender rehabilitation.

In dissecting the essence of corrections, it's essential to grasp that at its core, this sector operates on the foundational belief that individuals who have trespassed against societal norms can be rehabilitated and reintegrated into society. This concept is not merely aspirational but is grounded in decades of research and practice. Corrections encompass a broad range of functions and institutions including prisons, jails, probation, and parole systems, each designed to manage offenders in distinct stages of their rehabilitation journey.

The history of corrections is a mirror reflecting society's evolving values and theories concerning punishment and rehabilitation. From the punitive measures of the past to more rehabilitative approaches, the shift is evident in policies and practices. This evolution underscores the importance of understanding the past to effectively navigate the present and future challenges within this sector. The transformation from mere custodial care to more rehabilitative modalities signifies a shift towards prioritizing the reintegration of offenders back into society (Johnson, 2020).

Challenges in corrections are manifold and intricately linked to broader societal issues including mental health, substance abuse, and socioeconomic disparities. The high rates of recidivism, or the tendency of a convicted criminal to re-offend, is a stark indicator of the system's struggles to achieve its rehabilitative goals. Addressing these challenges requires an interdisciplinary approach, leveraging insights from psychology, sociology, and criminology to forge effective interventions.

The role of technology in corrections has been transformative, offering new tools for monitoring, rehabilitation, and management of offenders. From electronic monitoring devices to software that predicts the likelihood of reoffending, technology has the potential to enhance the effectiveness of correctional strategies. However, it also raises ethical and privacy concerns that warrant careful consideration.

Next, the role of community-based corrections cannot be overstated. Programs such as probation and parole play a crucial role in the reintegration of offenders into society. These alternatives to incarceration not only reduce the burden on prison facilities but also provide a supportive framework for the offender to make a positive transition back into the community.

Education and vocational training within the correctional system are vital for equipping inmates with the skills needed for successful reentry into society. Studies have shown that participation in educational and vocational programs significantly reduces recidivism rates by providing offenders with the tools necessary for socioeconomic stability post-release.

Mental health services within the corrections system have become increasingly pivotal, as a large proportion of the incarcerated population struggles with mental health issues. Providing adequate mental health care is not only a humanitarian necessity but also a strategic component in reducing recidivism by addressing one of its root causes.

The concept of restorative justice has gained traction, emphasizing healing for victims, offenders, and communities affected by crime. This approach seeks to go beyond the traditional punitive measures, offering pathways to reconciliation and a deeper understanding of the impacts of crime (Zehr, 2018).

The importance of staff training and development in the corrections field cannot be overstated. Correctional officers and staff are on the front lines, directly influencing the lives of inmates and the overall atmosphere within facilities. Investing in their training, particularly around de-escalation techniques and understanding mental health issues, is crucial for fostering an environment conducive to rehabilitation.

Looking towards the future, it is clear that corrections will continue to face significant challenges. These include managing the growing prison population, ensuring the humane treatment of inmates, and effectively facilitating their reintegration into society. Innovations in policy and practice, informed by ongoing research and the lessons of the past, are essential for addressing these challenges.

As students of criminal justice, you're encouraged to critically engage with the concepts of corrections and rehabilitation. Understanding the historical context, current practices, and future challenges will not only enrich your academic journey but also prepare you for meaningful contributions in this field. Let curiosity guide your exploration, and let compassion inform your perspectives on justice and rehabilitation.

The effective study of corrections in the context of criminal justice education requires a commitment to understanding the human stories behind the statistics and policies. It urges an appreciation of the delicate balance between safeguarding society and offering offenders meaningful opportunities for transformation and redemption. This balance is paramount in the quest for a more just and rehabilitative corrections system.

In conclusion, the corrections sector of the criminal justice system embodies the complex interplay between punishment and rehabilitation. It presents a unique blend of challenges and opportunities, requiring a thoughtful and informed approach. For students embarking on this educational journey, the study of corrections offers a profound opportunity to contribute to the evolution of a system at the heart of societal justice and human redemption.

The Importance of an Interdisciplinary Approach

In the realm of criminal justice, a single-dimensional approach falls significantly short of effectiveness and thorough understanding. As we delve deeper into the multifaceted structure of this field, the sheer complexity calls for a blend of disciplines, each offering unique insights and methodologies. This chapter underscores the critical relevance of integrating diverse academic fields to decode the criminal justice system in its entirety.

Criminal justice encompasses more than the straightforward application of law; it is an intricate web of societal reactions, ethical considerations, psychological underpinnings, and complex human behaviors. Acknowledging this, an interdisciplinary approach embroiders a richer, more nuanced tapestry of understanding. For instance, psychology proffers an understanding of criminal behavior, sociology examines the impact of crime on society while legal studies focus on the application and evolution of law. Together, these disciplines provide a holistic view, unveiling the depths beneath what appears merely as a surface.

The complexities of criminal justice systems worldwide demand a broad, adaptable perspective. International laws, human rights considerations, and transnational crimes such as human trafficking and cybercrime stretch the capacity of a single discipline to provide comprehensive solutions. Interdisciplinary studies equip students with the cognitive flexibility to navigate these challenges, fostering innovation and problem-solving skills that transcend traditional boundaries.

For a first-year college student stepping into the vast world of criminal justice, embracing an interdisciplinary approach is akin to equipping oneself with a multifaceted lens. This lens allows one to peer into the nooks and corners of the system, identifying not just the 'what' and 'how', but more importantly, the 'why'. Such an approach does not dilute focus but rather sharpens it, enabling a deeper engagement with the material.

Understanding the role of forensic science in criminal investigations exemplifies the necessity of biology and chemistry alongside criminological principles. Forensic evidence, such as DNA and ballistic reports, serve as critical links in solving crimes and prosecuting offenders. Their accurate interpretation, however, demands a comprehensive understanding of scientific principles.

The sociopolitical landscape also significantly influences the criminal justice system. Laws and policies do not exist in a vacuum; they are a response to societal norms, conditions, and changes. Political science and sociology thus become indispensable to understanding legislative processes, policy implications, and reform movements. An interdisciplinary perspective here illuminates the interconnectedness of legal systems with the societal fabric, guiding toward more empathetic and effective solutions.

Technology's burgeoning role in criminal justice further emphasizes the need for an interdisciplinary approach. Digital forensics, cybersecurity, and information technology have become pivotal in combating modern crimes, which are increasingly perpetrated through digital avenues. This intersection of criminal justice and technology necessitates a curriculum that is as fluid and dynamic as the subject itself, constantly evolving to incorporate the latest developments and tools.

Ethics and philosophy inject a moral compass into the study of criminal justice. They provoke critical thinking about justice, fairness, and the moral implications of legal decisions and policies. This philosophical grounding ensures that future professionals are not only skilled but also principled, fostering a justice system that upholds integrity and ethical standards.

The integration of communications studies into criminal justice education equips students with the skills necessary for effective advocacy, negotiation, and conflict resolution. Whether it's the eloquence required in courtroom advocacy or the sensitivity needed in victim assistance, effective communication is indispensable. It enhances transparency and trust within the system, contributing to its overall efficacy.

An interdisciplinary approach does not merely add knowledge; it amplifies comprehension and cultivates empathy. By understanding the psychological trauma of victims and the rehabilitative aspects of corrections, students can approach criminal justice with a balanced perspective, advocating for not just punishment but also healing and restoration.

In practical terms, this approach prepares students for the real-world challenges they will face as criminal justice professionals. It equips them with a versatile toolkit, enabling them to adapt to and address the multifarious aspects of crime and justice. The ability to draw upon different disciplines for insights and solutions is a powerful asset in a field as dynamic and impactful as criminal justice.

Moreover, engaging with multiple disciplines encourages collaborative learning and research. It fosters an academic and professional culture where sharing knowledge, methodologies, and perspectives is the norm. This collaboration is the bedrock of innovation, leading to more effective strategies for crime prevention, policy development, and community engagement.

In conclusion, an interdisciplinary approach in criminal justice education is not just beneficial; it's imperative. As we prepare the next generation of criminal justice professionals, it's crucial to instill in them the understanding that the strength of their impact lies not in the depth of knowledge in a single domain, but in the breadth of their understanding across multiple ones. This integrated approach is the key to unlocking a more just, compassionate, and effective criminal justice system.

For fresh faces in the collegiate world, let this chapter serve as an illuminating beacon, guiding you towards a richer, more encompassing journey through the criminal justice landscape. Embrace the diversity of disciplines as your arsenal in decoding the complexities of the system, for in this integration lies the path to true understanding and meaningful contribution.

Chapter 2: Setting Up for Success in Your First Year

Transitioning into the collegiate sphere, particularly within the rigorous domain of criminal justice, demands more than just academic readiness; it requires a mindset forged in the commitment to excellence and the resilience to navigate complexities. This chapter lays the foundation for this transformative journey, emphasizing that success is not merely a derivative of intelligence but the result of strategic planning, disciplined study habits, and active engagement with your academic community. Establishing effective study habits early on can significantly influence your academic performance, as noted by Zimmerman & Kitsantas (2002), who found a strong correlation between self-regulated learning strategies and academic success in higher education settings. Moreover, mastering time management skills becomes indispensable for criminal justice majors who must balance a demanding curriculum with the practical aspects of their studies (Macan, Shahani, Dipboye, & Phillips, 1990). Engaging with your courses goes beyond passive listening in lectures; it involves active participation, critical thinking, and applying theoretical knowledge to real-world scenarios, which enhances learning and retains interest (Freeman et al., 2014). By embracing these strategies, you set a solid groundwork for not just surviving but thriving in your first year and beyond, turning challenges into stepping stones for academic and personal growth.

Essential Study Habits

Entering the realm of higher education, especially within a field as demanding and intricate as the criminal justice system, necessitates a foundation of robust study habits. The transition from high school to college can be a formidable challenge, but it's also an opportunity to cultivate a set of skills that will not only ensure academic success but also prepare you for a rewarding career in this dynamic field. It's crucial to approach your studies with a strategic mindset and a disciplined work ethic.

One fundamental habit is to actively engage with the material. This means not just passively reading your textbooks but questioning, annotating, and discussing the content you're learning. This active engagement will help solidify your understanding and foster critical thinking skills, which are invaluable in the field of criminal justice.

Organization is another key to success. This involves both organizing your study space and your schedule. A clutter-free environment minimizes distractions and can help focus your mind on the task at hand. Similarly, a well-planned schedule ensures that you dedicate adequate time to each subject, while also balancing your studies with other essential aspects of your life. Remember, quality often trumps quantity when it comes to study time.

Setting specific, measurable, achievable, relevant, and time-bound (SMART) goals can tremendously improve your study efficiency. These goals can range from completing a set number of chapters each week to mastering a particular concept. By setting clear targets, you provide yourself with a roadmap to success, making your study sessions more focused and productive.

Don't underestimate the power of forming a study group. Collaborating with peers can provide new insights, broaden your understanding, and offer motivation. However, it's crucial to ensure that these groups remain focused and productive, avoiding the trap of becoming mere social gatherings.

Note-taking is an art that, when mastered, can significantly enhance your recall and understanding of complex topics. Develop a system that works for you, whether it's the Cornell method, mind mapping, or outline notes. Effective note-taking not only aids in comprehension but also serves as a valuable resource for exam preparation.

Regular review sessions are vital. Spacing out your study sessions and reviewing material over time greatly improves long-term retention. This technique, known as spaced repetition, leverages the psychological spacing effect, making it easier to remember information for exams and future applications in your career (Ebbinghaus, 1885).

Adopting a growth mindset is essential. Instead of viewing challenges and setbacks as insurmountable, view them as opportunities to learn and grow. The field of criminal justice is evolving, and success requires adaptability and a commitment to continuous learning and improvement.

Time management is another critical skill. Prioritize tasks, set aside dedicated study blocks, and avoid procrastination. Effective time management not only reduces stress but also ensures that you're making the most of your study time (Allen, 2001).

It's also essential to take care of your physical and mental health. Regular exercise, proper nutrition, and adequate sleep can greatly impact your concentration, memory, and overall academic performance. Moreover, mindfulness and stress management techniques can enhance your learning efficiency and well-being.

Utilize technology wisely. From study apps to digital textbooks, technology offers a plethora of tools to aid your studies. However, it's crucial to use technology judiciously and avoid distractions like social media when studying.

Seek feedback actively. Whether it's from professors, peers, or through self-assessment, feedback is invaluable for identifying areas of improvement and fine-tuning your study strategies. Constructive criticism is not a reflection of failure but a stepping stone towards excellence.

Be consistent. It's better to study a little each day than to cram all your studying into a few marathon sessions. Consistency helps to keep information fresh in your mind and reduces the stress of last-minute studying.

Finally, embrace curiosity. The field of criminal justice is vast and multifaceted, offering endless opportunities for learning and exploration. Let your curiosity guide your studies, and don't be afraid to delve deep into topics that intrigue you. This natural inquisitiveness will make your learning experience more enjoyable and rewarding.

Armed with these essential study habits, you're well on your way to success in your first year and beyond. It's a journey that will demand dedication, discipline, and perseverance, but the rewards—personal, academic, and professional—are immeasurable. Remember, the skills you're developing now will serve as the foundation for your future career in the criminal justice system, a field where your impact can truly make a difference.

Time Management Skills for Criminal Justice Majors

Embarking on the journey of a criminal justice major signifies the beginning of a rigorous yet rewarding academic endeavor. To navigate this path successfully, mastering time management is not just beneficial—it's essential. For students delving into the complexities of the criminal justice system, the ability to efficiently manage one's time can spell the difference between mere survival and flourishing in the academic environment.

First and foremost, understanding the magnitude of your coursework is crucial. Criminal justice studies entail a multidisciplinary approach, combining elements of law enforcement, legal studies, and corrections. This diversity requires a well-organized schedule to ensure that adequate time is allocated for each subject area. It's not just about squeezing in study sessions whenever there's free time; it's about creating a dedicated timetable that respects the depth and breadth of the curriculum.

A common pitfall for freshman is underestimating the preparation required for classes and assignments. A study by Locke et al. (1984) highlights the importance of goal setting and time management in enhancing academic performance. Setting specific, measurable, achievable, relevant, and time-bound (SMART) goals can bridge the gap between ambition and reality, enabling students to track their progress and adjust their strategies as necessary.

Effective time management also involves prioritization. Not all tasks are created equal, and recognizing this can significantly boost one's productivity. By identifying the most pressing assignments and allocating appropriate time to them, students can avoid the stress that comes with last-minute cramming sessions.

One particularly useful strategy is the Pomodoro Technique, a time management method that breaks work into intervals, typically 25 minutes in length, separated by short breaks. This technique can help maintain concentration and prevent burnout, which is especially beneficial when tackling complex legal theories or case studies.

Just as important as scheduling study time is the need for regular breaks. The brain needs downtime to process information, consolidate memories, and recharge for the next round of studying. Short breaks spent walking, exercising, or even just stretching can dramatically improve one's focus and productivity.

Another critical aspect of time management is learning to say no. The college offers a multitude of opportunities for involvement in clubs, sports, and other extracurricular activities. While these are valuable experiences, overcommitting can lead to academic difficulties. It's vital to gauge the time commitment required for these activities realistically and make informed decisions about what to pursue.

Utilizing technology can also enhance time management practices. There are numerous apps and software available designed to help with scheduling, task management, and productivity. Tools like Google Calendar or Todoist allow students to organize their tasks and deadlines effectively, ensuring that nothing slips through the cracks.

Procrastination is the arch-nemesis of effective time management. Overcoming the temptation to delay tasks requires discipline and motivation but is critical for success in criminal justice studies. Strategies to combat procrastination include setting small, manageable goals, creating a structured study environment, and rewarding oneself for completing tasks.

Collaboration with peers can also play a significant role in managing time efficiently. Study groups can offer mutual support, facilitate the sharing of resources, and provide diverse perspectives on complex topics. Engaging in discussions and collaborative learning can reinforce understanding and reduce the time needed to grasp difficult concepts.

Reflection and adjustment are fundamental to mastering time management. It's important to regularly review what strategies are working and which are not. Adjustments might be necessary as the semester progresses and the workload changes. Flexibility in one's approach to time management is key to finding what works best for an individual's learning style and schedule.

In summary, time management for criminal justice majors is not a one-size-fits-all skill. It requires a blend of strategic planning, discipline, and self-awareness. By setting clear goals, prioritizing tasks, taking regular breaks, and utilizing available resources, students can develop a framework for success that not only benefits their academic pursuits but also prepares them for future professional challenges in the criminal justice field.

Remember, the journey through criminal justice studies is as demanding as it is enriching. The mastery of time management empowers students to excel academically and professionally, making it an indispensable skill for those committed to making a difference in the field of criminal justice.

Engaging with Your Courses

Embarking on your journey through the criminal justice system in college is not merely about attending lectures and passing exams. It requires an active engagement with your courses, a commitment that bridges the gap between academic theories and real-world applications. This engagement is pivotal, shaping not only your academic success but your future career in criminal justice as well.

To fully immerse yourself in the study of criminal justice, start by cultivating curiosity. Curiosity drives inquiry, leading you to delve deeper into subjects that intrigue you. In a field as expansive as criminal justice, every topic from law enforcement tactics to correctional rehabilitation strategies holds layers of complexity waiting to be uncovered. Consider each course not just as a requirement to be completed but as an opportunity to expand your understanding of the intricate justice system that governs society.

Active participation is a cornerstone of engagement. During lectures, don't hesitate to ask questions that challenge the status quo or seek clarification on difficult concepts. Engaging with your professors and peers in thoughtful debates not only enriches your understanding but also fosters a dynamic learning environment. Additionally, participation in class discussions allows you to articulate your thoughts clearly, a critical skill in the practice of criminal justice.

Integrate theoretical knowledge with practical experiences. Seek opportunities to apply what you've learned in real-world settings, whether through internships, volunteer positions, or simulation exercises in your courses. These experiences not only enhance your learning but also provide a glimpse into the daily challenges faced by criminal justice professionals. Connecting theoretical concepts with practical applications prepares you for the complexities of working in the field.

Collaboration with classmates on projects and study groups can exponentially expand your learning horizon. Diverse perspectives can shed light on aspects of the criminal justice system that you might not have considered before. Collaborative learning environments encourage the exchange of ideas, critical thinking, and the development of teamwork skills essential in the criminal justice field.

Engage with your course materials. Beyond the required readings, explore additional resources such as academic journals, books, documentaries, and credible online content. This supplemental information can provide deeper insights into topics covered in your courses, sparking new interests and questions. Staying informed about current events in criminal justice is also crucial, as it allows you to connect classroom knowledge with ongoing societal issues.

Feedback from your professors is a valuable tool for improvement. Take the time to understand their comments and suggestions on your assignments and exams. If something isn't clear, requesting further clarification can unveil new ways to approach your studies.

Remember, feedback is not just about correcting mistakes but also about recognizing areas in which you excel and can further develop.

Time management is a vital component of engaging with your courses. Balancing coursework, extracurricular activities, and personal commitments can be challenging. However, developing a structured schedule that allocates dedicated study times for each class can help in staying organized and preventing last-minute cramming.

Adapting to different teaching styles and assessment methods is part of the collegiate experience. Each professor will have a unique approach to delivering content and evaluating your understanding. Being flexible and open to these variations can enhance your adaptability, a skill that is invaluable in the ever-changing field of criminal justice.

The use of technology has become integral in modern education. Familiarize yourself with the digital tools and platforms utilized in your courses. Online databases, academic software, and collaboration tools are not only resources for completing assignments but also means for expanding your learning beyond the traditional classroom.

Lastly, remember the importance of self-care during your studies. Engaging with your courses demands mental and emotional energy. Ensuring you are taking care of your well-being by getting enough rest, eating healthily, and finding time for relaxation is essential. A balanced lifestyle supports academic success and prepares you for the demanding career that lies ahead in criminal justice.

In conclusion, engaging with your courses in the field of criminal justice requires a multifaceted approach. It's about connecting with the material on a deeper level, actively participating in the learning process, and applying academic knowledge to real-world contexts. By embracing these strategies, you position yourself not just for academic success but for a rewarding career in shaping a just society.

Chapter 3: Navigating General Education Requirements

Navigating the landscape of general education requirements presents a unique opportunity for students in the criminal justice field to broaden their intellectual horizons and cultivate a versatile set of skills essential for their future careers. At the core of these requirements lies the intent to equip students with a well-rounded education that complements their specialized studies in criminal justice. By engaging with a diverse array of subjects, students not only enhance their critical thinking and analytical skills but also gain valuable insights into the societal, cultural, and ethical issues that intersect with the field of criminal justice. Developing a strategic approach to these courses, involving meticulous planning, effective resource utilization, and proactive engagement, can significantly enhance one's academic journey and professional preparedness. By integrating knowledge from various disciplines, criminal justice students can foster a more holistic understanding of the complex systems they will navigate in their careers, thereby optimizing their potential for success in both academic and professional realms. Indeed, mastering the art of navigating general education requirements is akin to laying a versatile and sturdy foundation upon which a successful career in criminal justice is built.

How These Courses Complement Your Major

The journey through your criminal justice major is undoubtedly punctuated with courses that, at first glance, might not seem directly relevant to your field of study. It's a pathway threaded with general education requirements that are not just box-checking exercises. These courses are integral building blocks, laying a foundation that complements your major, shaping you into a well-rounded professional poised to tackle the multifaceted challenges of the criminal justice system.

In essence, your foray into literature, philosophy, or natural sciences does more than just broaden your horizon; it equips you with a versatile set of tools. These subjects foster analytical thinking, critical reasoning, and a deepened understanding of the societal contexts in which the criminal justice system operates. For example, studying sociology can provide invaluable insights into the social structures and inequities that often underpin criminal behavior.

Similarly, psychology courses illuminate the complex interplay of individual behavior and cognitive processes, offering perspectives on why people commit crimes and how they can be rehabilitated. This understanding is crucial for any criminal justice professional aiming to implement more effective interventions and support systems within corrections, probation, and community services.

Mathematics and statistics courses, seemingly distant from the core interests of criminal justice, are cornerstones for developing the ability to analyze crime trends and evaluate the effectiveness of criminal justice policies and interventions. Mastery of statistical analysis enables you to discern patterns, test hypotheses, and contribute to evidence-based practices that are increasingly demanded in the field.

Communication skills, honed through courses in English and public speaking, are indispensable. Whether drafting reports, presenting cases, or negotiating with various stakeholders, the ability to communicate clearly and persuasively is paramount. These skills ensure that you are not just a passive actor within the system but a compelling advocate for justice and reform.

Historical studies offer a different kind of lens, providing a context for understanding the evolution of the criminal justice system. This knowledge is key to recognizing longstanding issues, evaluating progress, and advocating for meaningful changes. History teaches us not only about past mistakes but also about moments of triumph and reform that can inspire future pathways.

The study of ethics, a common component in general education curricula, is directly applicable to the myriad moral dilemmas faced by criminal justice professionals. From considerations about the death penalty to debates over surveillance and privacy, grappling with ethical questions prepares you to navigate the nuances of right and wrong in a legal context with integrity and compassion.

Political science courses enrich your understanding of the structure and functions of government, including the legislative underpinnings of the criminal justice system. This knowledge empowers you to engage more effectively with policy-making processes and to advocate for legal reforms grounded in social justice.

Science and technology courses, similarly, provide a backdrop for understanding the advancements in forensic science and digital investigation techniques that are revolutionizing the field. These classes ensure that you are not only cognizant of the current capabilities within criminal justice but are also prepared to adapt to and implement emerging technologies.

Environmental studies, while perhaps less connected, invite you to consider how environmental crimes and policies impact communities and the broader societal implications of crimes against the environment. This holistic approach underscores the interconnectivity of criminal justice with other societal concerns, promoting an ethic of sustainability and social responsibility.

Indeed, general education courses do much more than fulfill graduation requirements; they mold you into a thinker, a strategist, and a problem-solver. They instill a sense of curiosity and a desire for lifelong learning, traits that are indispensable in a field that is constantly evolving. The challenges faced by today's criminal justice professionals are diverse and complex, demanding not just specialized knowledge but also the creativity, empathy, and ethical grounding that a well-rounded education provides.

By incorporating these diverse courses into your study plan, you're not merely traversing academic checkpoints. You're laying a rich, multidisciplinary foundation that will support your aspirations within the criminal justice field. These courses, in their breadth and depth, complement your major in profound ways, preparing you for a career marked by innovation, compassion, and a steadfast commitment to justice.

In conclusion, as you navigate your general education requirements, view each course not as a hurdle but as a stepping stone. Each subject, each assignment, and each project is an opportunity to build upon your understanding of criminal justice, from multiple angles. Embrace these opportunities, and you'll find that these courses not only complement your major but are essential to your growth and success in the field.

Strategies for Success in Non-Major Courses

Navigating the sea of general education requirements can often feel like an ancillary part of your college journey, especially when your heart is set on mastering the intricate dance of the criminal justice system. Yet, these non-major courses are more than mere stepping stones; they are the bedrock upon which a well-rounded education is built. To excel, not just survive, in these courses demands a strategy that respects their role in shaping a holistic thinker poised to tackle the complexities of criminal justice.

The first strategy is to integrate, not segregate. Think of your education not as a collection of isolated units but as a cohesive whole. Courses in history, psychology, and sociology, for example, while not directly related to criminal justice, offer perspectives that enrich your understanding of societal dynamics crucial for a criminal justice professional. Approaching these courses with the mindset that they contribute to a larger picture can transform them from obligatory hurdles to integral components of your education.

Second, cultivate curiosity. It's the fuel that powers the pursuit of knowledge. Even if a subject seems distant from your major, curiosity can uncover fascinating links between disciplines. It might reveal, for instance, how philosophical theories on justice underpin legal systems or how behavioral psychology plays into criminal profiling. This intellectual curiosity not only makes learning more enjoyable but also deepens your engagement with the material, leading to better academic performance.

Third, hone your time-management skills. Balancing core courses with those in your major requires meticulous planning. Prioritize assignments and study time, but also be flexible; unexpected academic interests might arise from non-major courses that deserve exploration (Johnson & Carter, 2021). Effective time management ensures that you can give your best to every course, regardless of its direct relevance to your major.

Fourth, participate actively in class. Engagement isn't reserved for subjects you love. By participating in discussions and asking questions in all your classes, you deepen your understanding and make the material more memorable. This participation also signals to your instructors that you're invested in their course, which can be beneficial when you need support or guidance.

Fifth, leverage your major's perspective. Approach non-major courses by considering how their content can apply to criminal justice. Writing a paper for an English class? Explore themes of justice or moral quandaries in literature. Studying public speaking? Practice delivering arguments you might one day present in a courtroom. This method not only makes non-major courses more engaging but also reinforces your learning in your chosen field.

Sixth, seek out interdisciplinary projects. Whenever possible, choose topics for papers, presentations, and projects that allow you to bridge criminal justice with other fields. This not only demonstrates to your instructors your ability to think innovatively but also strengthens your analytical and research skills across diverse subjects.

Seventh, form study groups with peers from various disciplines. Engaging with students outside your major can provide fresh insights and approaches to learning. This diversity of thought can challenge your assumptions and stimulate intellectual growth, benefiting all your academic endeavors.

Eighth, develop a relationship with your professors. Even in non-major courses, professors can offer invaluable advice, mentorship, and professional connections. They can direct you to resources that intersect with your interests in criminal justice and offer perspectives you might not have considered.

Ninth, cultivate resilience. You might face subjects that are challenging or outside your comfort zone. Instead of shying away, embrace these challenges as opportunities to grow. The problem-solving and critical thinking skills you develop in these courses are directly transferable to your major studies and future career.

Tenth, reflect on your learning. Regularly take stock of what you've learned in non-major courses and how it applies to your understanding of criminal justice. This reflection not only reinforces learning but also aids in recognizing the value of a well-rounded education.

Eleventh, embrace technology. Utilize online resources, academic databases, and software tools recommended in non-major classes. These technological tools can enhance your research and productivity, not just for the course at hand but for all your academic pursuits.

Twelfth, practice academic integrity. The principles of honesty and ethical behavior apply across all your courses. Upholding these principles strengthens your character and professional preparedness for a career in criminal justice, where integrity is paramount.

Thirteenth, apply your learning in practical contexts. Look for opportunities to apply principles and theories from non-major courses in real-world settings, such as internships, volunteer roles, or part-time jobs. This application not only enriches your resume but also provides a deeper understanding of the interconnectivity between disciplines.

Fourteenth, pursue further reading and research. If a non-major course sparks your interest, delve deeper into the subject outside of class. This proactive approach to education enhances your knowledge base and demonstrates the initiative valued in criminal justice professions.

Fifteenth, and finally, maintain balance and wellness. The pursuit of academic excellence should not come at the expense of your health. Ensure that you allocate time for relaxation, exercise, and social activities. A balanced lifestyle supports academic success across all your courses and nurtures the resilience needed for a career in criminal justice.

In conclusion, the journey through non-major courses is not a detour but a critical component of your educational expedition. By adopting these strategies, you're not just passing classes; you're building the intellectual agility and depth of understanding that will distinguish you as a criminal justice professional. Embrace these opportunities to expand your horizon, and you'll emerge not only as a graduate but as a well-rounded scholar ready to contribute meaningfully to the field of criminal justice.

Chapter 4: Leveraging University Resources

In the grand narrative of your academic journey, mastering the utilization of university resources stands as a pivotal chapter. College, in its vastness, offers more than just lectures and textbooks; it's a conglomerate of tools, each designed to sculpt your path toward success, especially when studying complex fields like the criminal justice system. The library, often an underestimated haven, is not just a repository of books but a gateway to exhaustive online databases. These databases provide access to a plethora of academic journals, articles, and case studies, indispensable for deepening your understanding beyond the confines of your curriculum. Furthermore, the Writing Center emerges as a beacon of support, offering guidance to navigate through the intricate maze of APA formatting and enhancing your academic writing to meet the zenith of scholarly standards. Meanwhile, the role of a tutor extends beyond remedial help; engaging with someone who has navigated the path you're on can elucidate concepts that seem opaque, providing clarity and confidence in your academic endeavors. As you embark on this quest, remember, that the resources provided by your university are like the compass and map in the hands of an explorer; they are essential tools in discovering the vast and sometimes elusive treasure of knowledge.

The Library and Online Databases

Embarking on your academic journey in criminal justice demands a meticulous approach to research and study. Central to this pursuit is leveraging the comprehensive resources your university offers, notably the library and its online databases. The transition from high school to college can seem daunting, but the library, with its myriad resources, stands as a bulwark against the sea of academic challenges ahead.

At the heart of every university, the library serves not just as a repository of books but as a gateway to vast academic landscapes. Within its walls lie not only texts but also a plethora of digital resources, scholarly articles, and databases dedicated to the study of criminal justice. This is where your academic inquiries begin to find shape, guided by the wealth of resources at your disposal.

Understanding how to navigate online databases is crucial for a criminal justice student. These digital platforms offer access to a wide array of scholarly articles, research papers, and case studies essential for your studies. Databases such as JSTOR, LexisNexis, and the National Criminal Justice Reference Service provide focused, reliable information that can support your coursework, assignments, and research projects.

Unlocking the potential of these databases requires familiarity with search strategies. Boolean operators such as "AND", "OR", and "NOT" refine your search outcomes, enabling you to sift through vast amounts of information efficiently and effectively. It's a skill that develops with practice, and it's worth investing your time to master these search techniques early in your academic career.

Another vital aspect is understanding the relevance of peer-reviewed sources. The credibility of your work significantly hinges on the quality of your sources. Peer-reviewed articles have undergone rigorous evaluation by experts in the field, offering a level of reliability and academic integrity that non-reviewed sources cannot guarantee. This distinction is paramount when conducting research in criminal justice, where the accuracy and veracity of information bear direct implications on the interpretation of legal issues and policies.

Furthermore, the library is not an island. Librarians, those unsung heroes in the narrative of your academic success, possess a deep understanding of the research landscape in criminal justice. They can guide you through the intricacies of research methodologies, assist in identifying the most pertinent databases, and even aid in navigating the often complex maze of legal documents and reports.

One common oversight is underestimating the power of traditional library resources like books and academic journals in print form. While the digital age has revolutionized access to information, these physical resources remain invaluable. They provide depth and context that complement digital sources, offering insights and analyses that can enrich your understanding of the criminal justice system.

Maximizing the benefits of your university's library also involves utilizing its online portals and digital loan systems. Many libraries provide access to e-books, downloadable research papers, and online journals that are accessible from anywhere. This not only makes it convenient to study on your terms but also expands the horizons of your research possibilities.

Collaboration spaces in libraries serve as fertile ground for intellectual exchange and discussion. Group study rooms and quiet zones offer environments tailored to different study needs, whether it's collaborative project work or deep, focused research. Embracing these spaces can significantly enhance your learning experience and productivity.

The inscription to this endeavor is not without challenges. Information overload is a real concern in the digital age. Developing a critical lens through which to view search results, and discerning quality research from mere information, is a skill that is honed over time. It begins with understanding the hierarchy of sources, evaluating their credibility, and synthesizing them cohesively into your academic work.

Equally important is cultivating an ethical stance towards research. Plagiarism and intellectual dishonesty cast long shadows in academia. Learning to cite sources correctly not only respects the intellectual labor of others but also bolsters the integrity of your work. It's a testimony to your commitment to academic excellence and ethical scholarship.

Investing time in workshops and seminars offered by the library can vastly improve your research skills. These sessions are designed to enhance your competency in utilizing digital tools, managing bibliographies, and understanding the ethical dimensions of academic work. They equip you with the skills necessary to navigate the complexities of research in criminal justice.

Remember, the capability to research effectively sets the foundation for academic and professional success in the field of criminal justice. The library, with its resources and support mechanisms, is a critical ally in this journey. It's more than just a place to study; it's a hub of knowledge, a support network, and a resource center that can propel you towards academic excellence.

Embrace the opportunities that your university library offers. Delve into the online databases with curiosity and vigor. Let the resources available become the bedrock of your academic pursuits in criminal justice. The path to mastery is complex and fraught with challenges, but with the library as your compass, you are well-equipped to navigate this terrain.

As you forge ahead, remember that the essence of education lies in the quest for knowledge. At the heart of this quest is the library - a beacon of learning, guiding your steps through the intricate world of criminal justice.

Utilizing the Writing Center

The journey through your criminal justice major is not one you embark upon alone. As you delve into complex theories, case studies, and legal principles, one of the university resources at your beck and call is the Writing Center. It stands as a beacon for those who are navigating the academic waters of criminal justice, offering guidance, support, and a host of services designed to enhance your writing skills. This chapter sheds light on how you can leverage this valuable resource to your academic advantage.

First and foremost, the Writing Center is not merely a remedy for those struggling with writing but a resource for all students aiming to elevate the quality of their work. Whether you are drafting your first college essay or crafting a sophisticated research proposal, the Writing Center offers personalized feedback, practical writing strategies, and a supportive environment to refine your writing. Their goal is to make you a more confident and competent writer, a skill of paramount importance in the field of criminal justice.

Engaging with the Writing Center early in your academic career can set a solid foundation for future writing endeavors. By familiarizing yourself with their services, you can avoid the common pitfalls that many freshmen face when adjusting to college-level writing expectations. Remember, excellence in writing does not come overnight; it is a skill honed through practice, feedback, and perseverance.

One of the primary benefits of the Writing Center is its one-on-one tutoring sessions. These sessions are tailored to your specific needs, allowing you to work closely with experienced tutors on any aspect of your writing. Whether you need help organizing your thoughts, developing a thesis statement, or using evidence effectively, these tutors are there to guide you. They come from diverse academic backgrounds, including criminal justice, making them well-equipped to understand the nuances of your major.

Workshops and seminars are another cornerstone of the Writing Center. These group settings provide interactive learning experiences covering various topics, from grammatical accuracy to APA style, a critical component of writing in criminal justice. Attending these sessions not only sharpens your skills but also connects you with peers who may share similar challenges and goals.

For criminal justice students, mastering the art of research and academic writing is vital. The Writing Center plays a crucial role in this aspect by offering guidance on effectively integrating research into your papers. They can teach you how to synthesize information from multiple sources, a key skill when making arguments or analyzing criminal justice policies.

APA formatting is another area where the Writing Center can be invaluable. As most academic writing in criminal justice adheres to APA style, becoming proficient in this formatting guide is essential. The Writing Center provides resources and support to help you navigate the complexities of APA, ensuring that your papers meet the rigorous standards of academic writing.

Additionally, the Writing Center is an excellent resource for feedback on drafts. This feedback is not limited to grammar and syntax but extends to the coherence and flow of your argument, the clarity of your thesis, and the strength of your evidence. Such comprehensive feedback is instrumental in producing polished, compelling work that stands up to the scrutiny of professors and peers alike.

It's important to note that utilizing the Writing Center is a proactive step toward academic success. Rather than waiting until you are overwhelmed, make regular appointments throughout the semester to discuss your writing projects. This ongoing support can help you stay on track and continuously improve your writing skills.

The virtual support provided by the Writing Center is another aspect worth exploring. Online consultations and digital resources make it accessible to students who may have scheduling conflicts or prefer working from their own space. This flexibility ensures that all students have the opportunity to benefit from their services, regardless of their circumstances.

In the study of criminal justice, where the ability to communicate effectively and argue persuasively is invaluable, the Writing Center stands out as a critical ally. It not only aids in your academic development but also prepares you for the complexities of the criminal justice field, where writing plays a central role in nearly every facet.

Remember, the Writing Center is more than just a place to improve your writing. It's a place to grow as a student, thinker, and future criminal justice professional. By taking full advantage of this resource, you are not only investing in your academic success but also in your career in the criminal justice field. The skills you develop here will be ones you carry with you long after graduation, as you embark on a path to make significant contributions to society through your chosen profession.

As you proceed with your studies, keep in mind that the Writing Center is not just a resource; it's a community of learners, educators, and advocates dedicated to your success. Embrace it, and you will find that it can be one of the most rewarding aspects of your college experience.

In conclusion, the Writing Center is an indispensable resource for criminal justice majors, offering a breadth of services aimed at enhancing your academic writing. From personalized tutoring to workshops on APA style, it provides a comprehensive support system designed to elevate your writing skills. By actively engaging with the Writing Center, you are taking a significant step toward academic excellence and professional readiness in the field of criminal justice.

Finding and Working with a Tutor

Embarking upon the journey of higher education, particularly within the intricate tapestry of the criminal justice system, is akin to navigating a labyrinth. The complexities of law enforcement, court systems, and corrections demand more than just surface-level engagement. It's in this academic expedition that the value of a tutor becomes indispensable. A tutor can illuminate paths previously shrouded in obscurity, guiding students through difficult concepts and dense material. This segment delves into the process of finding and effectively working with a tutor, a crucial strategy in leveraging university resources for your success in studying criminal justice.

Finding the right tutor starts with a clear identification of your needs. As a criminal justice major, you may find yourself grappling with intricate legal theories one day and statistical analysis the next. The first step is to pinpoint the areas where you require the most assistance. Most universities offer tutoring services through their academic resource centers. These services are often included as part of your tuition, making them a financially viable option. When looking for a tutor, ensure they have a strong understanding of criminal justice. Their expertise can greatly affect how well they can help you grasp complex subjects.

Once you've identified a potential tutor, the next step is to establish clear goals for what you wish to achieve through tutoring. Is your aim to improve your grades, or do you seek a deeper understanding of certain concepts? Clear goals can help your tutor tailor their teaching methods to suit your needs. During your first session, it's beneficial to discuss these objectives. This conversation ensures both you and your tutor are aligned on expectations and outcomes.

Working with a tutor is a collaborative effort. Active participation is crucial. Prepare for your sessions by listing questions or topics you're struggling with. This preparation allows you to maximize the time with your tutor, focusing on overcoming your specific challenges. Don't hesitate to ask for clarification or further explanation on topics that aren't clear to you. Tutors appreciate engaged students, and your eagerness to learn can make the tutoring sessions more productive.

Regularly scheduled meetings with your tutor can provide structure and continuity in your learning process. Consistency is key to mastering complex subjects. Additionally, evaluating your progress with your tutor can shed light on your evolving understanding and reveal areas that might require further attention. Don't be discouraged by setbacks; they are an integral part of the learning curve. Instead, use them as stepping stones to deepen your knowledge.

The benefits of working with a tutor extend beyond academic improvement. Tutors can introduce you to study strategies and resources that you may not have encountered before. This can include ways to effectively research criminal justice topics, navigate academic databases, or approach writing assignments. These skills are not only beneficial academically but are also invaluable in the professional world.

Feedback from your tutor is a gift. Constructive criticism can help refine your thinking and approach to studying criminal justice. It's important to remain open-minded and receptive to feedback. Remember, the goal is to evolve in your understanding and application of the material. Your tutor's insights can guide you in this development.

Confidentiality and trust are paramount in a tutor/student relationship. The discussions you have and the work you share should remain private. This trust fosters an environment where you can freely express your thoughts and uncertainties without fear of judgment.

It's also valuable to remember that tutoring is not a one-way street. The insights you gain should be applied outside of the tutoring sessions. Applying what you've learned in your coursework and further reading consolidates the knowledge and deepens your understanding.

In the exploration of criminal justice, a tutor can be your guide, illuminating the path forward. However, the journey is yours to undertake. Your dedication, combined with the strategic support of a tutor, can significantly enhance your grasp of the subject matter. This partnership paves the way for academic and eventual professional success in the field of criminal justice.

In conclusion, leveraging the resources of a tutor can be a pivotal strategy in your academic journey. It requires a proactive approach in identifying your needs, finding the right tutor, and working collaboratively towards your academic goals. The journey through criminal justice studies is a challenging one, but with the right support, it can also be deeply rewarding. Remember, the goal is not just to pass your classes but to build a robust foundation of knowledge that will serve you in your future career.

Chapter 5: The ABCs of APA Formatting

As you venture deeper into your criminal justice studies, the precision and clarity of your scholarly writing will become paramount. APA formatting stands as a beacon, guiding your academic work toward excellence. This chapter aims to demystify the intricacies of APA style, ensuring your papers not only radiate scholarly integrity but also adhere to the strict guidelines that govern academic writing. You'll learn the essentials, from the basics of APA structure to the nuances of citing sources correctly and formatting different types of works. It's a journey that transcends mere rules, embedding itself in the fabric of your academic and professional ethos. Grasping APA isn't just about avoiding plagiarism or embellishing your bibliography; it's about embodying the rigor and precision that the field of criminal justice demands. Your ability to navigate these principles will distinguish your work, showcasing your dedication not only to the letter of the law but to the spirit of academic excellence as well. By mastering APA, you're not just learning a formatting style; you're honing a critical tool that will enhance your arguments, bolster your credibility, and sharpen your voice in the vast discourse of criminal justice.

Basics of APA Style

Embarking on the journey of higher education, particularly in a field as dynamic and complex as criminal justice, requires not only an understanding of the subject matter but also a mastery of the tools that convey this understanding. Among these, the American Psychological Association (APA) Style stands out as a critical framework for writing and research within the social sciences, including criminal justice studies. APA Style, with its precise guidelines for formatting, citation, and referencing, facilitates the clear communication of ideas and supports the creation of scholarly work that is both credible and accessible.

The essence of APA Style extends beyond mere formatting—it's about creating a standardized language that ensures scholars across disciplines can share and evaluate knowledge without ambiguity. This function is pivotal, especially for freshmen embarking on their academic and professional journeys in criminal justice. A thorough grasp of APA Style not only enhances your ability to document sources correctly but also bolsters your academic integrity, distinguishing your work in the scholarly community.

At its core, APA Style emphasizes clarity, precision, and a focus on the content rather than the form. This means that while formatting is important, the primary goal should always be to communicate your ideas as effectively as possible. For instance, the use of headings in APA Style helps organize and structure the content, making complex topics in criminal justice more digestible for the reader. Similarly, the precise citation of sources enables writers to substantiate their arguments, drawing on a wealth of existing research and evidence.

Navigating APA Style begins with understanding the basic formatting rules. This encompasses everything from the correct use of margins and fonts to the organization of the reference list. Such details, though seemingly minor, play a significant role in maintaining the scholarly rigor and visual coherence of your work. For example, using the prescribed Times New Roman, 12-point font size, and double-spacing all text ensures that your document adheres to the conventions expected in academic settings.

Moreover, APA Style mandates the inclusion of four major sections in your paper: the title page, abstract, main body, and references. Each serves a distinct purpose and must be formatted according to specific guidelines. The title page, for instance, serves as the face of your work, providing essential information like the paper's title, your name, and your institutional affiliation—all of which signal the seriousness and authenticity of your research.

The abstract, though brief, is no less critical. This concise summary of your paper's key points provides readers with a snapshot of your research, including its scope, methodology, results, and conclusions. Crafting a compelling abstract can draw readers into your work, highlighting its relevance to the field of criminal justice.

In the main body of your paper, APA Style's emphasis on clarity and order becomes most evident. Here, the organization of ideas, the use of proper citation to avoid plagiarism, and the employment of clear, concise language are paramount. These components ensure that your arguments are presented logically, supported by evidence, and easily understood by your intended audience.

When it comes to citing sources, APA Style provides a rigorous yet straightforward system. Whether quoting directly or paraphrasing, it is imperative to give credit where it is due. The in-text citation system allows readers to locate the source of specific ideas or data, underscoring the research's foundation on established knowledge.

The reference list is the cornerstone of APA Style. This comprehensive compilation of all sources cited in your work not only serves to credit the original authors but also provides readers with the resources to explore these topics further. Formatting each entry correctly, according to APA guidelines, is crucial for maintaining the integrity and utility of your reference list.

Adhering to APA Style also means staying updated with its latest edition, as the guidelines are periodically revised to reflect advances in scholarly communication. Keeping abreast of these changes ensures that your work remains current and maintains its credibility among scholars and professionals alike.

For freshmen entering the field of criminal justice, mastering APA Style might seem daunting at first. However, it's a journey worth embarking on. The precision and rigor it demands mirror the very qualities needed to excel in criminal justice studies—and, by extension, in the field itself. It's a symbol of your commitment to academic integrity, your respect for the work of fellow scholars, and your dedication to the pursuit of knowledge.

Remember, proficiency in APA Style does not emerge overnight. It is cultivated through consistent practice, attention to detail, and, most importantly, a willingness to learn and adapt. As you progress in your studies, you'll find APA Style to be an invaluable ally, one that enhances the clarity and impact of your work, facilitating a deeper engagement with the criminal justice discourse.

In closing, consider APA Style as more than a set of rules to follow. It's a scholarly language that, when mastered, opens doors to the vast world of academic research and discourse. Embrace it with enthusiasm and diligence, and let it be a tool that sharpens your academic and professional capabilities in the criminal justice field. As you embark on this intellectual journey, remember that the precision and structure APA Style brings to your work are reflections of your clarity of thought and purpose.

As you forge ahead, let the meticulousness demanded by APA Style inspire you to approach your studies and future career in criminal justice with the same level of integrity and excellence. The journey is as rewarding as the knowledge you'll gain, shaping you into not just a student of criminal justice, but a scholar who contributes meaningfully to the field.

Citing Sources Correctly

In the pursuit of mastering the criminal justice system through academic rigor, one cannot overstate the importance of citing sources correctly. At the heart of academic writing, especially in the field of criminal justice, lies the foundation of responsible scholarship—acknowledging the contributions of others. This is where the American Psychological Association (APA) formatting guidelines shine as a beacon for students navigating the complex seas of academic writing. Citing sources correctly is not merely a technical skill but a mark of scholarly integrity and respect for both the creators of original ideas and the readers who seek to trace the paths of research and discussion.

Understanding how to cite sources correctly in APA format requires an appreciation for the details that make each citation meaningful and useful. Each citation tells a story of research, development, and collaboration. Whether citing a groundbreaking study on criminal behavior or a comprehensive review of correctional facility strategies, the way you cite these sources adds value to your work by situating it within the broader academic conversation.

At the foundation, citing sources correctly involves recognizing the various types of sources you may encounter. From peer-reviewed journal articles and books to interviews, websites, and even social media posts, each has a place in research with its specific way of being cited according to APA guidelines. This variety demonstrates the expansive nature of research and the multiple lenses through which one can examine criminal justice phenomena.

When citing a single author, the format (last name, YYYY) sets the stage for a clear, concise acknowledgment of the work. This simplicity, however, belies the complexity and depth of the research being credited. Similarly, when the work of two authors is integrated into your paper, the format (last name & last name, YYYY) signifies a partnership in the creation of knowledge, reminding us of the collaborative nature of academic endeavors.

For sources authored by three or more individuals, the format changes slightly to (last name et al., YYYY), encapsulating the collective effort in a streamlined manner. This economy of language in APA formatting helps maintain the flow of your writing while ensuring each contributor's work is acknowledged.

Citations are not just placeholders; they are essential threads in the tapestry of scholarly work. They guide readers through the maze of research, leading them to the sources of ideas and evidence that support or challenge your arguments. A correctly cited source stands as a pillar of credibility, enhancing the trustworthiness of your work.

Beyond the basic formats, the nuances of citing sources in APA style extend to how one incorporates quotes, paraphrases, and summaries. Quoting directly from a source requires precision and acute attention to detail, ensuring that the original meaning is preserved while seamlessly integrating it into your work. Paraphrasing and summarizing, on the other hand, require a deep understanding of the source material, allowing you to reiterate the ideas in your own words while maintaining the original intent.

The digital age brings its challenges and opportunities to citation practices. Digital sources, such as websites and online journals, require a slightly different approach, taking into account the URL or DOI and the date of access, acknowledging the fluid nature of online content. This adaptability in citing digital sources reflects the evolving landscape of research and the increasing importance of online resources in the field of criminal justice.

An incorrectly cited source, or worse, a failure to cite, can mar the integrity of your work, casting a shadow over your dedication and respect for the principles of academic honesty. Plagiarism, the specter that haunts academic writing, is effectively countered through diligent and accurate citation of sources, protecting both the writer and the original creators of the content.

For students embarking on the journey of mastering APA formatting, the path may seem strewn with challenges. Yet, it is through these very challenges that one develops not only a technical skill but a deeper appreciation for the ethics of research and writing. Correctly citing sources is a testament to your commitment to engaging in meaningful, responsible scholarship.

In closing, citing sources correctly is an act of respect—respect for the past research that paves the way for new insights, respect for the community of scholars, practitioners, and policymakers who contribute to the understanding of criminal justice, and respect for the integrity of the academic discipline itself. As you delve deeper into your studies, let the precision and care with which you cite your sources reflect your dedication to contributing constructively and honorably to the field of criminal justice.

Remember, your journey through academic writing is not a solitary one; it is a shared endeavor enriched by the voices of countless researchers, thinkers, and writers whose work you will cite. In recognizing their contributions, you join a community dedicated to the pursuit of knowledge and the advancement of justice in society.

Embrace the discipline of APA formatting with enthusiasm, for it is a key that unlocks the door to scholarly writing and a reflection of your commitment to the rigorous and respectful study of criminal justice.

APA Formatting for Different Types of Works

As you embark on your journey through the fascinating world of criminal justice, you'll quickly discover the indispensable role of effective communication in the field. Among the most crucial tools at your disposal will be your proficiency with APA formatting. This format, developed by the American Psychological Association, is not merely a set of arbitrary rules but a beacon guiding the clarity, precision, and reliability of your scholarly work. In this section, we'll illuminate the process of applying APA style to various types of works, equipping you with the knowledge to navigate the terrain of academic writing with confidence.

When it comes to journal articles, the heart of academic discourse, APA formatting shines in its attention to detail. Here, every author's name, the year of publication, the article title, the journal name, volume number, and page number are meticulously recorded. This rigorous treatment allows readers to trace the genesis of ideas and engage deeply with the discourse. For a journal article, the format might look like this: Author(s). (Year). Title of the article. *Title of the Journal, Volume number(Issue number)*, pages. It's a format that respects the lineage of knowledge while inviting further scholarly exploration.

Books, with their expansive narratives and complex arguments, are treated with equal reverence. In APA format, the author's name, the publication year, the book title, and the publisher's information are keenly cataloged. This format - Author(s). (Year). *Title of the book*. Publisher - serves not only as a citation but as an homage to the work's contribution to the body of knowledge. Whether it's a groundbreaking treatise on criminal psychology or an authoritative text on law enforcement tactics, the APA format provides a framework that honors the author's endeavor.

Conference proceedings, the crucibles of emerging ideas and debates, require a nuanced approach. APA format captures the essence of these scholarly gatherings by including the author's name, the date of presentation, the title of the work, and details about the conference. This meticulous cataloging - Author(s). (Year, Month). Title of paper. In *Name of the conference*, Location - not only guides readers through the intellectual ferment of these gatherings but also highlights the evolving nature of academic discourse.

Theses and dissertations, the pinnacle of academic rigor, are accorded great respect in APA style. For such works, the format - Author(s). (Year). *Title of thesis*. (Degree). Institution - serves as a testament to the scholar's contribution to their field. It's a format that not only acknowledges the arduous journey of academic inquiry but also places the work within the larger tapestry of scholarly endeavor.

Web resources, with their ease of access and ubiquity, pose unique challenges. APA format meets these challenges by including the author's name, the date of publication, the title of the work, and the URL. This approach ensures that digital works are accorded the same level of scrutiny and respect as their print counterparts, acknowledging the shifting landscapes of academic research.

When dealing with audiovisual materials, an area of growing importance in criminal justice studies, APA style adapts with flexibility. Citing these sources includes the creator's name, the year of release, the title of the work, and additional publication details. This recognition of diverse formats underscores the APA's commitment to inclusivity in scholarly communications.

Through its meticulous structuring, APA formatting empowers you to cite sources with precision across various mediums. But beyond the mechanics of citation lies a deeper philosophy. APA formatting is not just a method but a ritual that honors the integrity of academic work, nurtures the growth of ideas, and fosters a community of trust among scholars. As you delve into criminal justice studies, mastering APA formatting is not merely a practical skill but a rite of passage into the scholarly community.

Remember, this journey through APA formatting is more than learning a set of rules; it's about embracing a scholarly ethos that values clarity, precision, and respect for the intellectual contributions of others. Whether you're examining the nuances of criminal behavior, the intricacies of the legal system, or the challenges of corrections and rehabilitation, your ability to communicate effectively and ethically is paramount. By adhering to APA standards, you're not only enhancing the quality of your work but also contributing to the collective endeavor of truth-seeking that defines the academic community.

As you proceed, keep in mind that the specific examples provided here are your guiding stars as you navigate the vast ocean of academic writing. The practice of meticulously formatting your work according to APA guidelines may seem daunting at first. However, like any skill worth acquiring, it becomes second nature with practice. The eventual mastery of this skill will significantly enrich your academic endeavors, making your work accessible, credible, and engaging to your peers and the broader community of scholars dedicated to the study of criminal justice.

In conclusion, the meticulous application of APA formatting across different types of works is more than an academic requirement; it is a tribute to the pursuit of knowledge and an essential tool in the dissemination of ideas. By embracing this format, you are not only preparing yourself for success in your criminal justice studies but also honoring the scholarly tradition that underpins the quest for justice in society. Let the principles of APA formatting guide you in your scholarly pursuits, inspiring your work with clarity, rigor, and integrity. As you wield these principles with confidence, you'll find that they not only open the doors to academic success but also pave the way for a meaningful contribution to the field of criminal justice.

Chapter 6: Writing Excellence in Criminal Justice

Embarking on the journey of mastering written communication within the realm of criminal justice is both a necessity and a virtue for the aspiring student. The meticulous nature of crafting coherent, compelling essays and reports mirrors the investigative diligence required in law enforcement, legal analysis, and policy formulation. Understanding your assignment sets the cornerstone of this venture, requiring a clear grasp of objectives and expectations. Engaging in robust research and note-taking strategies is not merely an academic exercise but a preparatory step in cultivating the analytical acumen necessary for dissecting complex legal and ethical dilemmas. Through crafting your argument, you're not just laying down a thesis but weaving a narrative that holds the power to inform, persuade, and instigate action. The iterative process of revising and editing your work, therefore, transforms from a chore into a critical reflection of your evolving thought process and understanding of criminal justice principles. As you hone your written expression, let the guidance of academia meld with your passion for justice, allowing your words to become conduits of change and enlightenment in a society that yearns for both safety and fairness.

Understanding Your Assignment

Embarking on the journey of mastering criminal justice involves not only comprehending the complexities of the law but also excelling in how these theories and practices are communicated through writing. Your assignments are the bridge between theoretical knowledge and practical application, necessitating a clear understanding right from the outset. This section delves into how to unfurl the layers of your assignment, ensuring that your academic endeavors in criminal justice are both enlightening and exemplary.

First and foremost, it's crucial to read the assignment prompt thoroughly. Sounds straightforward, doesn't it? Yet, many students skim over the details, missing out on critical instructions or misinterpreting the requirements. Each word in the prompt has been carefully selected to guide your research and writing process. By dissecting the prompt, you're laying the groundwork for a comprehensive response that aligns with the educator's expectations.

Identifying the type of assignment is your next step. Are you crafting an argumentative essay, a research paper, or perhaps a case study analysis? Each format demands a distinct approach; for instance, an argumentative essay calls for a persuasive stance backed by evidence, while a case study analysis might require a detailed examination of criminal justice practices and their outcomes. Recognizing the nature of your task is pivotal in structuring your research and writing accordingly.

Clarifying the assignment's objectives cannot be overstated. What is the instructor aiming to assess through this task? It could be your ability to apply theoretical frameworks to real-world scenarios, your critical thinking skills, or perhaps the depth of your research. Understanding these goals shapes your study strategy and ensures that the hours you invest in reading, note-taking, and writing propel you toward success.

Setting a realistic timeline is another cornerstone of conquering your assignment. Procrastination might be a sly companion, but it's certainly not a friend of academic excellence. Breaking down the assignment into manageable tasks—such as initial research, drafting, revising, and final proofreading—gives you a roadmap that is less daunting and more achievable, ensuring quality work without the last-minute rush.

Once you have a grasp on what the assignment entails, it's time to delve into the research phase. Here, quality trumps quantity. While the internet is an ocean of information, not all sources are created equal. Selecting peer-reviewed articles, reputable news outlets, and authoritative books is essential (Flanagan, 2006). This curated approach to research underpins your arguments with credibility, an essential aspect of scholarly writing, especially in a field as critical as criminal justice.

As you embark on this journey, don't overlook the importance of engaging with diverse perspectives. The field of criminal justice is vast and multifaceted, encompassing views from law enforcement, legal experts, sociologists, psychologists, and more. Each perspective offers unique insights that can enrich your understanding and, by extension, your assignment.

An essential aspect often overlooked is the value of drafting an outline. An outline is more than a formal requirement; it's a strategic map for your thought process, ensuring that your argument flows logically from one point to the next. This clarity of structure is particularly important in complex fields like criminal justice, where arguments must be built on solid evidence and clear reasoning.

Equally vital is the critical evaluation of your sources. In criminal justice, where laws and societal norms are constantly evolving, the relevance and recency of your sources can significantly impact the strength of your argument. This discerning approach to source material not only demonstrates your analytical skills but also anchors your assignment in the present context.

When it comes to writing, clarity and conciseness are your allies. The field of criminal justice is inherently complex, and your ability to articulate ideas clearly is paramount. This doesn't mean oversimplifying complex concepts but presenting them in a manner that's accessible and engaging to your intended audience, which, in this case, is your instructor and possibly your peers.

Another crucial aspect is adherence to academic standards, notably APA formatting. The meticulous citation of sources not only lends credibility to your work but also demonstrates your respect for intellectual property—a core value in the academic and professional worlds (Williams & Tollett, 2018). This commitment to academic integrity is a hallmark of excellence in criminal justice studies.

Don't hesitate to seek feedback throughout the writing process. Whether it's from peers, instructors, or academic support services within the university, constructive criticism is invaluable. It offers fresh perspectives on your work, highlights areas for improvement, and reinforces your strengths. This iterative process of writing, receiving feedback, and revising is integral to refining your academic voice.

As you near the completion of your assignment, the revision process becomes paramount. It's tempting to view your first draft as a finished product, especially after investing significant effort. However, excellence in writing—especially within the demanding field of criminal justice—requires a commitment to refinement. This stage is not merely about correcting grammatical errors but enhancing the coherence, flow, and persuasiveness of your argument.

Finally, embracing a mindset of continual learning and improvement will stand you in good stead. The field of criminal justice, with its dynamic nature and societal impact, offers endless opportunities for intellectual and personal growth. Each assignment, with its challenges and triumphs, contributes to your development not just as a student but as a future practitioner committed to justice and societal well-being.

In conclusion, understanding and excelling in your criminal justice assignments demand a synthesis of critical reading, strategic research, clear writing, and an earnest engagement with the complexities of the law and society. This endeavor, while challenging, is immensely rewarding, paving the way for a fulfilling academic and professional journey in criminal justice.

Research and Note-taking Strategies

Embarking on your criminal justice studies involves more than just understanding the law; it entails mastering the art of research and note-taking. These skills are fundamental in dissecting the vast expanse of criminal justice literature, theories, and case studies you'll encounter. Effective research begins with knowing where to look and how to sift through an ocean of information to find those golden nuggets of knowledge. Let's dive into the strategies that can help you excel in your criminal justice academic journey.

Firstly, identifying reputable sources marks the cornerstone of any research project. The internet, while a trove of information, is also a minefield of misinformation. Prioritize scholarly databases and libraries as your information source. Resources like JSTOR, Google Scholar, and your university's digital library facilitate access to peer-reviewed journals, articles, and books that are crucial to your studies (Smith & Jones, 2019).

Developing a systematic approach to your research is as essential as the sources you utilize. Begin by defining clear, concise research questions. What are you trying to discover? What specific aspect of criminal justice are you delving into? These questions will guide your research process, ensuring it remains focused and efficient.

Once you've established a clear research directive, it's time to gather your data. While amassing information, it's pivotal to keep meticulous notes. Note-taking isn't merely jotting down facts; it's about recording insights, questions, and connections between pieces of information. This nuanced approach to note-taking will serve you well when you begin synthesizing your research into coherent arguments.

Categorize your notes based on themes or subjects. This strategy aids in the organization of your thoughts and findings, making it easier to retrieve information when needed. Employing digital tools and software for note-taking can enhance this process, allowing you to tag and search your notes efficiently.

Skimming through material can be beneficial in the initial stages of your research to determine relevance. However, once you've pinpointed valuable sources, in-depth reading is crucial. Look for main ideas, supporting evidence, and how these relate to your research questions. Highlighting and annotating as you go can help solidify your understanding and recall of the material.

Another critical aspect of research and note-taking is the evaluation of sources. Not all information is created equal. Assess the credibility of your sources by considering the authors' qualifications, the publication date, and the outlet of publication. This scrutiny ensures that your research is based on reliable, up-to-date information that can withstand academic scrutiny.

As you compile information, it's important to keep track of your sources. Accurate citation is not only critical for avoiding plagiarism but also for building a viable argument in your papers. Familiarizing yourself with APA formatting early on will make this process much smoother.

Effective research and note-taking also involve making connections between different sources and ideas. Look for patterns, themes, and discrepancies in your notes. Drawing these connections early on can guide the direction of your research and help formulate a compelling thesis for your papers.

Don't hesitate to revise your research questions as you delve deeper into your subject matter. The research process is dynamic; new findings might prompt you to adjust your focus or explore new avenues. Flexibility in your research approach allows you to adapt and ensures your work remains relevant and insightful.

Collaboration can also enrich your research process. Discussing your findings with peers or professors can provide new perspectives and insights you might not have considered. Moreover, they can suggest additional resources or methodologies to enhance your research.

Finally, remember that research and note-taking are skills honed over time. Be patient with yourself, and don't shy away from experimenting with different strategies to find what works best for you. Each project offers a new opportunity to refine your approach and develop your proficiency.

As you move forward in your criminal justice studies, integrating these research and note-taking strategies will be instrumental in achieving academic success. They are the tools that will enable you to navigate the complexities of the criminal justice system, providing a solid foundation for your future endeavors in this field.

Crafting Your Argument

In the realm of criminal justice, the strength of your argument can often be the lynchpin of your academic and future professional success. Crafting a compelling argument requires not just a firm grasp of the facts at hand, but a deep understanding of how to weave those facts into a narrative that is both convincing and engaging. This involves a blend of critical thinking, rigorous research, and a dash of creativity – a combination that can seem daunting at first but is within your grasp with the right approach.

First, understand the issue you are tackling from all angles. A thorough investigation of the topic at hand is crucial. This isn't just about accumulating as many sources as you can find. It's about identifying the core of the debate, the various viewpoints that exist within it, and the evidence that supports or refutes these perspectives. This process, foundational in the study of criminal justice, hinges on an ability to critically assess the validity and reliability of data.

Equally important is the development of a thesis statement. This statement should not just declare your position but also outline the main points that will support your stance. Think of your thesis as the backbone of your argument; every claim you make, and every piece of evidence you present, should somehow reinforce this central premise.

Logical organization is next. Your argument should flow seamlessly from one point to the next, with each paragraph building on the argument presented before it. This is where a detailed outline becomes an invaluable tool. By plotting out your main points ahead of time, you can ensure a logical progression of ideas, making your argument more coherent and, thus, more persuasive.

Using evidence effectively is perhaps the most critical aspect of crafting your argument. In the context of criminal justice, evidence can range from statistical data and case law to expert testimony and anecdotal accounts. However, it's not just about piling on information. You must be selective, using only the most relevant and convincing evidence to back up your claims. Additionally, each piece of evidence needs to be linked back to your thesis, reinforcing your argument at every turn.

Counterarguments should not be overlooked. Addressing opposing views does not weaken your position; rather, it demonstrates your comprehensive understanding of the topic and enhances the credibility of your argument. Critically engage with these counterarguments, refute them with evidence, or acknowledge their validity while explaining why your stance still holds.

Clarity and conciseness are your allies. In the pursuit of academic rigor, it's easy to fall into the trap of using overly complex language or adding unnecessary information. However, clear, straightforward writing is most effective at conveying your points to the reader. Every sentence should serve a purpose. If it doesn't advance your argument, consider revising or removing it.

Stylistically, remember that variation in sentence structure keeps your writing dynamic. While the substance of your argument is paramount, the delivery also matters. A mix of short, impactful sentences and longer, more descriptive ones can make your argument more engaging.

Your conclusion is where you drive your argument home. It should not simply restate your thesis but rather synthesize the information you've presented into a compelling final insight. The conclusion is your opportunity to leave a lasting impact on your reader, to underscore the importance of your argument within the broader context of criminal justice studies.

Throughout this process, feedback is invaluable. Share drafts with peers, instructors, or mentors. Fresh eyes can offer perspective on unclear points, logical gaps, or areas in need of further development. Incorporate this feedback thoughtfully, refining your argument to make it as strong as possible.

Ultimately, the art of argumentation in criminal justice is about more than just academic assignments; it's a skill that will inform your professional contributions to the field. Whether drafting legal documents, preparing for courtroom presentations, or developing policies, the ability to present a clear, convincing argument is indispensable.

Remember, crafting an argument is a skill honed over time. Each essay, research paper, and project presents an opportunity to practice and improve. Embrace these chances, challenge yourself to think critically, and don't be afraid to engage in complex debates. With dedication and practice, your argumentation skills will grow stronger, serving you well throughout your academic journey and into your career in criminal justice.

Revising and Editing Your Work

Once the journey of crafting your argument and articulating your insights on the criminal justice system on paper begins, true artistry emerges in the revising and editing process. This crucial phase transforms your initial drafts into compelling, clear, and academically rigorous pieces of writing. It's here that your abilities to critically think, analyze, and refine your work are put to the test, embodying the pursuit of excellence in criminal justice scholarship.

Starting with revision, it's important to understand the distinction between revising and editing. Revision implies a deep, comprehensive examination of the content, organization, and coherence of your writing. It's an opportunity to ask yourself if your arguments flow logically if the evidence you've provided sufficiently supports your claims, and if you've effectively communicated your understanding of the topic at hand.

Editing, on the other hand, focuses on the fine details of your work: grammar, punctuation, spelling, and adherence to style guides, particularly APA format, which is predominant in the social sciences, including criminal justice (American Psychological Association, 2020). While editing might seem less daunting than revising, it requires a meticulous eye and a thorough understanding of language rules and formatting standards.

One of the initial steps in revising your work should be to set it aside for a short period. Whether it's a few hours or a couple of days, distancing yourself from your writing allows you to return with a fresh perspective, making it easier to spot inconsistencies and areas for improvement that you might have missed before.

When it comes time to review your work, consider reading it aloud. This method can spotlight awkward phrasing or convoluted sentences that disrupt the flow of your narrative. It's a simple yet effective tool for ensuring that your writing is not only clear but also engaging to your audience.

Peer review is another invaluable aspect of the revision process. Sharing your work with classmates or mentors provides you with feedback from those who may have a different perspective or insight into the topic. Be open to critiques, as they often uncover areas for enhancement that weren't previously apparent.

As you incorporate feedback and make adjustments, focus on strengthening your argument. Ensure that each paragraph supports your thesis and that transitions between sections are smooth and logical. In essence, every sentence should serve a purpose to substantiate your claims and advance your overall argument.

Turning to the technicalities, proper citation is critical in the editing phase, especially for a discipline rooted in facts and research such as criminal justice. Ensure every source is credited accurately according to APA guidelines— a task that underscores your integrity and dedication to scholarly standards (American Psychological Association, 2020).

Finally, the importance of proofreading cannot be overstated. While spell-check tools are convenient, they're far from infallible. A careful, line-by-line review is indispensable for catching typographical errors that could detract from your paper's professionalism and credibility.

Remember, revising and editing are not one-time tasks but iterative processes that might necessitate several rounds of review to achieve writing excellence. It's a testament to the adage that great writing isn't born, it's built—piece by painstaking piece.

In sum, the journey from an initial draft to a polished piece of writing in criminal justice is both challenging and rewarding. It calls for patience, persistence, and an unwavering commitment to excellence. By embracing this process, you not only enhance your writing skills but also deepen your understanding of the complex and dynamic field of criminal justice.

In writing, as in criminal justice, the devil lies in the details. Paying close attention to both the broad strokes of your argument and the minutiae of grammar and citation can elevate your work from good to exemplary. Such dedication to excellence sets the foundation for success not only in academia but also in the multifaceted world of criminal justice practice and policy.

Remember, the essence of writing in criminal justice is to communicate complex ideas with clarity, precision, and authority. Whether dissecting landmark court rulings, analyzing crime trends, or evaluating policy proposals, your ability to effectively revise and edit your work will stand you in good stead.

Armed with these insights and strategies, you are now better equipped to refine your work to the highest standards of scholarly excellence. Let this undertaking be not just an academic exercise, but a labor of passion, a testimony to your commitment to understanding and improving the criminal justice system through rigorous inquiry and scholarly discourse.

Chapter 7: Beyond the Classroom: Experiential Learning

Embarking on the path of experiential learning provides a vibrant tapestry on which the theoretical knowledge acquired in the confinement of classroom walls is enriched and applied in real-world settings. Grounded in the belief that learning is most impactful when it is interactive and situated within authentic contexts (Kolb, 1984), this chapter delves into the myriad of ways students of criminal justice can extend their education beyond traditional academic settings. Internships, particularly, stand as a cornerstone of this experiential edifice, offering unparalleled immersion into the practical facets of the criminal justice system. They not only bolster theoretical constructs with practical application but also illuminate career pathways through firsthand exposure (Sweitzer & King, 2009). Furthermore, volunteering opportunities knit the fabric of community engagement with academic pursuits, fostering a sense of civic responsibility and providing insight into the grassroots level of criminal justice operations (Stanton, Giles, & Cruz, 1999). Lastly, networking within the criminal justice field can significantly amplify the experiential learning sphere, embedding students within a professional community that is ripe with mentorship, collaboration, and opportunity exploration. The synthesis of these experiential dimensions cultivates a learning environment where academic and practical realms converge, equipping students with a holistic, nuanced understanding of the criminal justice system.

Internships and Their Value

As you embark on the transformative journey through your college years, studying the vast and intricate field of criminal justice, it's imperative to recognize that learning extends far beyond the four walls of a classroom. At the core of a truly comprehensive education in criminal justice lie internships, vital opportunities that allow you to immerse yourself in the real-world applications of theories and concepts discussed in lectures. This chapter delves into the invaluable role internships play in shaping your understanding, skills, and prospects within the criminal justice realm.

Internships serve as a bridge between theoretical knowledge and practical experience, offering a tangible context to the abstract principles taught within your courses. In the dynamic field of criminal justice, where laws and societal expectations evolve, the importance of staying abreast of such changes can't be overstated. Internships, therefore, provide a live platform for observing and participating in the application of current laws, justice procedures, and ethical considerations (Miller & Hess, 2021).

Engagement in an internship not only enhances your understanding of criminal justice but also significantly amplifies your employability. In a sphere where experience often parallels or even surpasses academic credentials, internships provide the hands-on experience that employers value. They're a testament to your initiative, demonstrating your willingness to go beyond the required academic curriculum to prepare for your future career (Stockdale et al, 2022).

Another facet of internships is their capacity to foster networking. The criminal justice field is notably community-oriented and connections made during your internship can serve as crucial links for future job prospects. These professional relationships provide mentorship, advice, and insight, often opening doors to opportunities that might otherwise remain inaccessible.

Internships also offer a unique perspective on the diversity of career paths within the criminal justice system. Whether your interests lie in law enforcement, legal practice, corrections, or rehabilitation, internships can provide a firsthand look at potential career routes. This exposure is invaluable in shaping your academic and professional decisions, helping you to align your studies and eventual career with your strengths and interests.

It's essential, however, to approach these opportunities with strategic intent. Selecting an internship should be a process as deliberate and thoughtful as choosing a course or a major. Consider the areas of criminal justice that most interest you, the skills you wish to develop, and the type of organization that aligns with your career goals.

Preparation is key to securing and succeeding in an internship. Utilizing your university's resources, such as the career services center or your academic advisor, can provide you with a competitive edge. They can assist with resume building, interview preparation, and identifying valuable internship opportunities that match your career aspirations.

During your internship, the focus should be on learning and growth. Taking initiative, asking questions, and seeking feedback can transform a routine internship into a profound learning experience. It is an opportunity to build your competency, confidence, and perhaps most importantly, your character. The challenges faced and overcome during internships often lead to profound personal and professional development.

Reflection upon your internship experience is equally vital. Internships can affirm your chosen path or inspire a change in direction. Engage in reflective practices, such as journaling or discussions with mentors, to glean insights from your experiences. This reflective process is invaluable for integrating your internship experiences with your academic studies and career aspirations.

Furthermore, internships provide a real-world context that can enrich your academic work. The practical experiences gained can serve as examples in essays, contribute to class discussions, and inspire research projects. This synergy between practical and academic learning enhances both, making your education richer and more relevant.

However, it's important to understand that not all internships will be a perfect fit. Challenges and mismatches in expectations may arise. Treat these situations as learning opportunities, a chance to hone your adaptability, and problem-solving skills, and to learn what truly motivates you within the criminal justice field.

To maximize the value of internships, it's crucial to maintain a balance between your academic responsibilities and your internship. Effective time management and communication with your academic advisors and internship supervisors are essential to ensure both your studies and your practical experience are complementary, not conflicting.

In the pursuit of internships, equality and access are significant considerations. Strive to identify and pursue opportunities that promote diversity, equity, and inclusion, recognizing the imperative of these values within the criminal justice system itself. Your internship should not only advance your career prospects but should also reflect a commitment to justice and equity.

In conclusion, internships are not just a supplement to your education in criminal justice; they are a pivotal, integral part of it. They bridge the gap between theory and practice, enhance employability, provide networking opportunities, and offer insights into your personal and professional potential. As you navigate through your academic journey, let internships illuminate your path, guiding you to a fulfilling career in the vast labyrinth of criminal justice.

Volunteer Opportunities

Transcending the boundaries of traditional classroom learning, volunteer opportunities offer a profound pathway for criminal justice students to engage directly with the core subjects they study. The vibrant world beyond the lecture halls and textbooks is filled with chances to apply theoretical knowledge in practical settings, enriching one's understanding and passion for the criminal justice system.

In this era of academic pursuit, where theoretical knowledge meets real-world application, volunteering stands as a beacon of experiential learning. It's not just about gaining insight into the criminal justice system; it's about immersing oneself in the community's heartbeat, understanding its challenges, and contributing to meaningful change. For freshmen embarking on this journey, volunteering can serve as a window into the complexities and nuances of the criminal justice landscape.

The significance of volunteer work in the context of criminal justice education cannot be overstated. Institutions and organizations ranging from local police departments to non-profit advocacy groups frequently offer volunteer positions that allow students to witness criminal justice principles in action. This hands-on exposure complements academic studies, providing a tangible context to abstract theoretical concepts.

Moreover, the benefits of volunteering extend far beyond mere observation. Students who engage in volunteer work develop critical skills such as problem-solving, communication, and ethical reasoning. These competencies are invaluable across all criminal justice careers, from law enforcement to legal advocacy. Furthermore, volunteering fosters a sense of civic responsibility and social awareness, particularly in areas of community policing, victim support services, and rehabilitation programs.

Identifying suitable volunteer opportunities requires careful consideration of one's interests, career aspirations, and academic goals. Students are encouraged to seek opportunities that align with their passions within the criminal justice field. Whether it's working alongside law enforcement, supporting rehabilitation efforts, or advocating for legal reform, the right volunteer experience can significantly impact a student's educational journey and professional trajectory.

Engagement with volunteer opportunities also presents a unique advantage in the realm of networking. Building relationships with professionals in the field can open doors to internships, job offers, and mentorship opportunities. This networking aspect underscores the importance of approaching volunteer experiences with professionalism and dedication, as these contacts could become key influencers in one's career.

One must approach volunteering with an open mind and a desire to learn, not just from professionals but also from the communities served. This humility and willingness to understand different perspectives are essential in developing a well-rounded approach to criminal justice.

For students considering volunteer work, it's advisable to start by consulting with their academic advisors or the college's career services. These resources can provide valuable information on finding opportunities that match one's academic schedule and interests. Additionally, student-led organizations and clubs focused on criminal justice issues often partner with local agencies and can be a good source of volunteer leads.

When embarking on a volunteer opportunity, it's essential to set personal learning objectives. What does one hope to achieve or learn from this experience? Reflecting on this question can help maximize the benefits of volunteering, ensuring that the experience contributes meaningfully to both personal growth and academic success.

Incorporating volunteer experiences into one's academic portfolio can also be advantageous. Documenting the skills gained, challenges encountered, and insights obtained during volunteer work can showcase a student's practical understanding of the criminal justice system to future employers or graduate studies programs.

It's important to remember that volunteering is a two-way street. While students gain invaluable experience, they also contribute to the functioning and improvement of the criminal justice system. This reciprocity underscores the transformative potential of volunteer work, both for the individual and for society.

Lastly, the impact of these volunteer experiences is not just limited to career prospects. They often instill a lifelong commitment to social justice and community service. This foundation, built in the early stages of one's academic journey, sets the stage for a rewarding career dedicated to public service and the betterment of society.

In conclusion, volunteer opportunities in the criminal justice field offer a rich tapestry of learning experiences that extend far beyond the conventional classroom setting. For freshmen who are just beginning their journey, these opportunities can illuminate the path forward, revealing the intersections between academic study and real-world impact. Thus, engaging in volunteer work is not just a supplement to one's education—it's a cornerstone of a holistic criminal justice education that empowers students to make a difference in the world.

Networking in the Criminal Justice Field

In our exploration of the expansive landscape of criminal justice, a pivotal component often overlooked in the conventional classroom setting is the art and science of networking. As you embark upon the terrain of this critical aspect of your education, it's essential to understand that the relationships you cultivate now can significantly influence your future within the field of criminal justice.

Networking, in its essence, extends beyond the mere exchange of business cards or LinkedIn connections. It involves a strategic effort to build meaningful relationships with professionals, educators, and peers who share a connection to your field of interest. For a student in criminal justice, leveraging these connections can unlock opportunities, provide insights into various career paths, and even facilitate mentorships that guide your academic and professional journey.

Consider the conferences, seminars, and workshops that frequent the academic calendar. Each presents a unique platform for engaging with thought leaders, innovators, and seasoned professionals who have navigated the complexities of the criminal justice system. Presence at these gatherings, coupled with an active engagement, opens doors to dialogues that can sow the seeds for enduring professional relationships.

The concept of informational interviews further underscores the value of networking. Reaching out to practitioners within your area of interest for informal discussions can demystify aspects of the profession that might seem opaque from the outside. Such interactions not only broaden your understanding but also allow you to make informed decisions about your career trajectory.

Social media platforms and professional networking sites stand as modern conduits for connecting with industry professionals. Building a robust professional profile that reflects your academic achievements, projects, and areas of interest can attract the attention of potential mentors and employers. Engaging with content related to criminal justice, sharing insights, and participating in relevant discussions can elevate your profile within professional circles.

Internships, as discussed in the preceding section, serve not only as invaluable experiential learning opportunities but also as fertile grounds for networking. Through internships, you're placed into the heart of the work environment, where daily interactions with professionals provide a firsthand understanding of the inner workings of the criminal justice system. These experiences can solidify into professional relationships that persist beyond the tenure of the internship.

Volunteering offers another avenue for networking. By contributing your time and skills to causes and organizations aligned with your interests in criminal justice, you can demonstrate your commitment to the field, all while building a network of contacts who can vouch for your dedication and abilities.

Peer networking, while sometimes underestimated, carries tremendous potential. Your fellow students today stand as the future professionals of tomorrow. Developing a strong network amongst your peers can lead to collaborative opportunities, mutual support, and shared growth throughout your career.

Faculty members represent another critical network. Professors and instructors, with their wealth of knowledge and industry contacts, can provide mentorship, recommend participation in projects, and introduce students to professionals within their networks. Cultivating relationships with faculty can lead to research opportunities and career guidance.

Professional associations in the criminal justice field offer membership to students, often at a reduced rate. These organizations can be a goldmine for networking opportunities, industry news, professional development resources, and employment postings. Active participation in these associations can significantly expand your professional network.

The process of networking should be approached with a clear strategy. Set goals for what you wish to achieve through your networking efforts, whether it's learning more about a particular career path, securing a mentor, or identifying internship opportunities. Tailoring your approach to these goals can lead to more fruitful outcomes.

Professionalism and etiquette play pivotal roles in networking. First impressions count, and maintaining professionalism in your interactions, correspondence, and social media presence is paramount. A respectful and courteous approach opens more doors and leaves a lasting positive impression.

Follow-up and follow-through are key components of successful networking. After making a new contact, reach out with a thank you note, express your appreciation for their time, and articulate any takeaways or next steps you plan to pursue as a result of your conversation. Demonstrating your attentiveness and interest can solidify a fledgling connection into a meaningful professional relationship.

Networking, in summary, is an art that, when mastered, can significantly enhance your educational and professional journey in the field of criminal justice. It's a symbiotic process of giving and taking, learning and sharing, aimed at fostering relationships that support mutual growth and success. As you proceed in your studies, keep in mind that the connections you make today could very well shape the trajectory of your career tomorrow.

Chapter 8: Technology in Criminal Justice Studies

As we delve into Chapter 8, it's evident that the landscape of criminal justice studies is continually reshaped by burgeoning technological advancements. The integration of technology within this discipline is not just a passing trend; it's a profound evolution that's enhancing both the efficacy and efficiency of criminal justice processes. From digital databases that streamline research to sophisticated software tools that simulate crime scene investigations, technology offers unprecedented potential for students and professionals alike. Understanding and mastering these technological tools and concepts is paramount for students aspiring to thrive in a modern criminal justice career. The necessity of digital literacy for research, analysis, and presentations cannot be understated, acting as the bedrock for navigating the complex digital terrain encountered in modern criminal justice studies. Moreover, the advent of essential software and tools not only empowers students with the capabilities to conduct thorough investigations but also equips them with the skills to present their findings compellingly and professionally. This chapter aims to prepare students for the digital demands of their field, emphasizing the utility and application of technology in criminal justice studies, setting a foundational stone for success in this digitally-driven era

Essential Software and Tools

Embarking on a journey through the complex and evolving world of criminal justice requires more than just determination and intellectual curiosity. It demands a set of digital tools and software that can enhance understanding, streamline research, and polish communication. For budding criminal justice scholars, familiarizing yourself with these essential tools is not just beneficial; it is indispensable for success.

At the forefront of essential software for criminal justice students is data analysis software. With the increasing importance of big data in law enforcement and policy making, students must become adept at using software like IBM's SPSS or the open-source alternative, R. These tools offer powerful functionalities for statistical analysis, helping students to dissect and understand crime patterns, predict outcomes, and make data-driven arguments.

Another vital tool in the criminal justice arsenal is Geographic Information Systems (GIS) software, such as ArcGIS. GIS technology enables the visualization, analysis, and interpretation of data in ways that reveal relationships, patterns, and trends through maps. This proficiency can be instrumental in crime mapping, tracking the spread of illicit activities, and planning law enforcement resource allocation efficiently.

For those delving into the legal aspects of criminal justice, legal research databases like Westlaw or LexisNexis are indispensable. These platforms provide access to a vast repository of legal documents, case law, statutes, and legal journals. Mastery of these databases not only enriches a student's research but also prepares them for the rigorous research work required in legal careers.

Given the importance of communication in this field, proficiency in document creation and presentation software, such as Microsoft Office Suite or Google Workspace, is essential. Crafting compelling reports, creating engaging presentations, and managing data spreadsheets are skills that students will frequently draw upon throughout their studies and professional careers.

To collaborate effectively on projects and assignments, familiarity with project management and collaboration tools like Trello, Slack, or Microsoft Teams is highly beneficial. These platforms facilitate group projects, streamline communication, and help in managing deadlines and tasks in an organized manner.

For advanced research, qualitative data analysis software such as NVivo offers functionalities to analyze unstructured or qualitative data like interviews, open-ended survey responses, articles, and social media content. This tool is especially useful for students undertaking thesis projects or participating in research that requires deep qualitative analysis.

Ethical hacking and cybersecurity tools, while more niche, are becoming increasingly relevant in a world where cybercrime and digital forensics are at the forefront of criminal justice challenges. Tools and platforms like Kali Linux introduce students to the fundamentals of information security, an area of growing importance in law enforcement agencies.

In the realm of case management and crime reporting, software such as ARMS (Automated Record Management Systems) can provide practical insights into the administrative side of law enforcement operations. Understanding the workflow and data management within such systems can offer invaluable practical experience for students.

To stay updated with the latest research and developments in the field, RSS feed aggregators or academic journal databases like JSTOR and Google Scholar are crucial. They allow students to subscribe to pertinent journals, keeping them informed about new studies, theories, and findings in criminal justice.

Lastly, the role of digital literacy cannot be overstated. In addition to specialized software, a basic understanding of digital security practices, online research methodologies, and the ability to navigate and discern the credibility of web-based resources are foundational competencies every student should possess.

The integration of these tools and software into your study routine will not only facilitate a deeper understanding of the criminal justice system but also equip you with the skills and competencies sought after in the modern workforce. As you move forward in your studies, remember that mastering these tools is a progressive journey—one that parallels your academic and professional development in criminal justice.

As you familiarize yourself with these essential software and tools, consider each as a stepping stone towards not just academic excellence, but towards becoming a well-rounded professional in the field of criminal justice. The ability to leverage technology effectively is a distinguishing factor that can set you apart in a competitive landscape.

In conclusion, the landscape of criminal justice is increasingly digital and data-driven. The software and tools outlined here form the bedrock of a robust educational foundation in this field. As you progress in your studies, continuously seek to expand your digital toolkit, always be mindful of the role each tool plays in your development as a future criminal justice professional. Embrace these tools with curiosity and diligence, for they are your allies in deciphering the complexities of the criminal justice system.

Digital Literacy for Research and Presentations

In criminal justice studies, mastering the art of digital literacy becomes indispensable for students aiming to illuminate the complex layers of the law, criminology, and social justice through their research and presentations. As we delve deeper into the digital age, the necessity to sift through an ocean of information quickly and accurately, discern credible sources, and effectively utilize digital tools for compelling presentations, cannot be overstressed. This chapter focuses on equipping you with the digital literacy skills essential for excelling in criminal justice research and presentations.

At the outset, understanding the concept of digital literacy extends beyond mere internet navigation and word processing. It encompasses a multitude of competencies including information retrieval, evaluation of sources, digital communication, and the ethical use of digital content. For criminal justice students, this means not only finding relevant statutes, case laws, or academic papers but also evaluating their relevancy, authenticity, and applicability to the research question or topic at hand.

Embarking on research, a plethora of digital databases and online libraries beckon. Platforms such as JSTOR, Google Scholar, and the specific National Criminal Justice Reference Service (NCJRS) are treasure troves of academic papers, legal documents, and reports. Leveraging these resources effectively begins with precise query formulation. Employing Boolean operators - "AND", "OR", "NOT" - refines search results, bringing you closer to the most relevant literature. Remember, the precision of your search terms directly influences the quality of your findings.

However, finding the information is only half the battle. The next step involves critically evaluating the sources. In criminal justice, the veracity and credibility of information cannot be taken lightly, as it has real-world implications. Assess the publication date, the author's credentials, and the publishing body to establish the reliability of the information. Peer-reviewed articles and government reports typically provide a strong foundation for academically rigorous research.

With a plethora of information at your fingertips, organization becomes key. Digital tools such as Zotero or Mendeley can aid in managing your sources, enabling you to create a structured library of references. These tools also come with the added advantage of integrating with word processors for seamless citation and bibliography creation, adhering to APA guidelines - a staple in criminal justice writing.

Transitioning from research to presentation, digital literacy entails the effective communication of your findings. Tools like PowerPoint, Prezi, or Canva allow for the creation of visually engaging presentations that can captivate your audience. Yet, the tool is only as good as the operator. Understanding the principles of good design, such as the rule of thirds, complementary color schemes, and font readability, is crucial in crafting presentations that are not only informative but also aesthetically pleasing.

Moreover, the skill of digital storytelling becomes particularly relevant in the field of criminal justice, where cases and theoretical perspectives can be detailed in a narrative format, making the information more relatable and digestible for the audience. Utilizing a combination of text, visuals, and audio elements can transform a traditional presentation into a compelling story, drawing your audience into the narrative you are weaving.

Yet, with great power comes great responsibility. The ethical considerations in using digital content — be it images, videos, or documents — must be carefully heeded. Always ensure you have the right to use third-party content or attribute it correctly according to fair use policies and copyright laws. This not only safeguards against plagiarism but also upholds the integrity of your work.

In addition to the credibility of academic work, digital literacy also encompasses the aspect of cybersecurity. As criminal justice students, protecting the confidentiality and integrity of sensitive information should be second nature. Practicing safe browsing, securing personal data, and being aware of phishing scams are basic but critical habits to cultivate.

Venturing further into presentations, mastering the art of public speaking in a digital context also holds relevance. Online presentations, webinars, or virtual conferences have become mainstays in academic and professional environments. Here, understanding the nuances of digital communication — maintaining eye contact through the camera, mastering the audio-visual tools at your disposal, and engaging with a virtual audience — are skills that augment the impact of your presentation.

As we advance through our academic and professional journeys, the landscape of digital literacy continues to evolve. Staying abreast of the latest digital trends, tools, and resources can provide a competitive edge in the field of criminal justice. This means being adaptable, continuously learning, and applying new skills in research and presentations.

To summarize, digital literacy stands as a cornerstone of academic success in criminal justice studies. From efficiently navigating databases for research to engagingly presenting complex ideas, the competencies encapsulated within digital literacy are manifold. As you progress, remember that the journey of enhancing digital literacy is ongoing, reflecting the dynamic nature of both technology and criminal justice itself.

In conclusion, as you immerse yourself in the depths of criminal justice studies, let your quest for digital literacy be both methodical and inspired. The digital age presents an unprecedented opportunity to glean insights, share knowledge, and impact discussions within the criminal justice sphere. Harnessing digital tools and resources with proficiency and integrity will not only elevate your academic endeavors but also prepare you for the multifaceted challenges of the criminal justice field.

Chapter 9: Preparing for Advanced Courses

As you progress through your journey in the criminal justice major, the complexity and depth of your courses will naturally increase. To excel in these advanced courses, it is crucial to build firmly upon your foundational knowledge, integrating key themes and theories of criminal justice with practical application and analysis. Comprehensive preparation involves more than just memorizing facts; it requires synthesizing and critiquing information from various sources, including landmark case studies and seminal research. DioGuardi. (2016) underscores the importance of critical thinking skills in navigating complex legal scenarios and justice system mechanics, emphasizing that a deep understanding of theoretical frameworks significantly enhances practical decision-making and problem-solving abilities. Equally, mastering advanced research methodologies is vital. Familiarity with diverse data collection and analysis techniques allows for a critical evaluation of criminal justice practices, enabling students to contribute meaningfully to the field. Furthermore, engaging actively with current issues and debates in criminal justice through academic journals and discussions fosters a dynamic learning environment that primes students for success in both their academic and future professional careers. This chapter thus serves as a bridge, guiding you from the foundational principles laid in earlier courses to the rigorous analysis and independent research required in upper-level classes. Through a blend of theoretical mastery and practical skills development, you'll be well-equipped to tackle the challenges of advanced criminal justice coursework, preparing you for a successful career in the field.

Key Themes and Theories in Criminal Justice

Embarking on the study of criminal justice invites you into a complex world that straddles the theoretical and the practical, the abstract and the concrete. It's a field where the pursuit of justice intersects with dynamic societal forces, and understanding its foundational themes and theories is crucial for any student aiming to excel. This section delves into several key areas that are indispensable in preparing for advanced courses in criminal justice.

At its core, criminal justice studies revolve around understanding the nature of crime, the motivations behind criminal behavior, and the societal reactions to crime. One of the primary theories you'll encounter is the "Classical School" of criminology, which posits that individuals have free will to choose criminal or lawful solutions and that deterrents can be structured to prevent crime (Beccaria, 1764). This theory lays the groundwork for much of the legal framework in criminal justice systems today.

Contrasting with the Classical School is the "Positivist School," which argues that criminal behavior arises from factors outside an individual's control, such as biological, psychological, and social influences (Lombroso, 1876). This perspective has fueled the development of rehabilitation programs and has significant implications for corrections and criminal justice policy.

Understanding the theories of crime causation, including the sociological theories like "Social Disorganization Theory" (Shaw & McKay, 1942) and "Strain Theory" (Merton, 1938), enriches your ability to analyze criminal behavior. It introduces a framework for examining how societal structures and pressures contribute to criminal behavior, shifting the focus from individual to community-level interventions.

Another fundamental theme in criminal justice is the concept of "justice" itself. What constitutes justice in a diverse and dynamic society? Exploring theories of justice, including retributive, restorative, and distributive justice, allows for a deeper understanding of the goals and challenges within the criminal justice system. These concepts challenge students to envision more equitable and effective responses to crime.

The ethical considerations within criminal justice cannot be overstated. Professionals in this field face moral dilemmas daily, navigating the thin line between upholding the law and ensuring justice. Exploring ethical theories and their application in law enforcement, the judiciary, and corrections is vital for developing a moral compass as a future criminal justice professional.

The impact of globalization on crime and criminal justice practices is another critical area of study. In an increasingly interconnected world, crimes like human trafficking, cybercrime, and transnational terrorism demand a global perspective on criminal justice education and practice. This theme prepares students for the complexities of fighting crime that transcends borders.

Technological advancements have also reshaped the landscape of criminal justice, from developments in forensic science to the use of big data in predicting crime patterns. Understanding the role and implications of technology is essential for navigating the future of criminal justice work.

Lastly, the pursuit of equity and social justice in criminal justice practices underscores much of the study in this field. Examining issues of racial bias, disparities in sentencing, and the impact of policies on marginalized communities is fundamental. This examination not only reflects the ongoing societal dialogue about justice but also challenges students to be agents of change.

As you delve into these themes, you will find that each one opens up new avenues for exploration, questioning, and growth. The interdisciplinary nature of criminal justice studies calls for an integration of knowledge from psychology, sociology, law, and public policy, enriching your understanding and preparing you for the complexities of the field.

Preparing for advanced courses in criminal justice, therefore, means grappling with these themes and theories not just intellectually but also personally. They invite you to reflect on your values, challenge your perspectives, and inspire you to envision your role in creating a more just society.

What's critical is that as you progress in your studies, remember that the realm of criminal justice is ever-evolving. Theories that are dominant today may be questioned tomorrow, and new themes may emerge in response to shifting societal factors. Staying curious, open-minded, and engaged is essential. Your journey through the study of criminal justice is not just about acquiring knowledge; it's about becoming a thoughtful, informed, and proactive participant in the field.

In embracing these themes and theories, you're laying the groundwork for a fruitful and impactful career in criminal justice. You're not just preparing for advanced courses; you're stepping into a larger conversation about what justice means in the 21st century and how it can be achieved. The road ahead is challenging, but for those passionate about making a difference, it's incredibly rewarding.

So, as you move forward, approach your studies with a mix of humility and ambition. The field of criminal justice calls for nothing less. It's a field where you have the potential to impact lives, shape policies, and contribute to the societal good. The themes and theories you're about to dive into are your maps in this endeavor—use them well.

Remember, the journey into criminal justice is as much about learning from the past and understanding the present, as it is about shaping the future. You're not just a student of criminal justice; you're an evolving part of its narrative. Let that inspire you as you pave your path through this complex, challenging, and ultimately rewarding field.

Building on Foundation Knowledge

As freshmen in college, embarking on the study of the criminal justice system requires a solid base upon which to build. This base, or foundation knowledge, is crucial for understanding the complexities you'll encounter in advanced courses. Just as a skyscraper relies on its sturdy foundation to rise confidently into the sky, your academic and professional future in criminal justice depends on the strength of the groundwork laid during your initial year of study.

Foundation knowledge in criminal justice encompasses an understanding of its three main components: law enforcement, court systems, and corrections. Each of these segments introduces distinct yet interconnected disciplines, theories, and practices that are essential for a comprehensive grasp of the field. As you delve deeper into your studies, this triad becomes the lens through which more specialized knowledge is filtered and understood.

The interdisciplinary approach highlighted in earlier discussions isn't just academic rhetoric; it's a pragmatic strategy for navigating the complexities of criminal justice. The law doesn't operate in isolation from sociology or psychology; therefore, a well-rounded foundation must include insights from these and other disciplines. This cross-pollination of ideas fosters innovative thinking and problem-solving skills, which are invaluable in advanced studies and beyond.

One might wonder how best to fortify this foundation. Engagement with your courses through active participation, relentless curiosity, and critical thinking is key. The study habits and time management skills covered previously are the tools with which you carve out your niche in the vast expanse of criminal justice. This proactive engagement ensures that the knowledge gained sticks, creating a durable foundation.

Besides the classroom, leveraging university resources plays a significant role in building upon your foundational knowledge. Libraries and online databases are treasure troves of scholarly articles, books, and case studies that can deepen your understanding of criminal justice topics. Similarly, the writing centers can help sharpen your ability to articulate complex ideas clearly and concisely, a skill that's paramount in advanced coursework.

APA formatting, though seemingly a technical aspect of writing, serves a greater purpose in the academic journey of a criminal justice major. Mastery of APA style reflects a student's attention to detail and respect for the integrity of scholarly communication. This discipline in citing sources correctly prevents the erosion of foundational knowledge by ensuring that information is accurately relayed and acknowledged.

As you move towards more specialized studies, the importance of research and note-taking strategies cannot be overstated. These skills allow you to sift through the vast amounts of information available, identifying what is most relevant and valuable for your study. This methodical approach to gathering information bolsters your foundation, ensuring that it is built on reliable and pertinent knowledge.

Moreover, crafting your argument in papers and assignments is a practice of critical thinking and persuasion, both of which are central to the practice of criminal justice. This skill is cultivated over time, starting with simpler assignments and building complexity as you progress. It's this capability to construct and defend arguments that form a significant portion of the foundational knowledge needed for advanced studies.

The revision and editing process is equally part of this foundational building. It teaches resilience and the understanding that excellence comes from revision and continuous improvement. This iterative process not only enhances your academic work but also prepares you for the critical analysis required in advanced criminal justice courses.

Experiential learning through internships and volunteer opportunities further solidifies your knowledge base. Real-world experience provides context to the theoretical concepts learned in class, creating a more well-rounded understanding of the criminal justice system. This practical engagement is invaluable as it prepares you for the application of advanced theories and concepts in real-world scenarios.

Networking within the criminal justice field introduces students to the perspectives and insights of seasoned professionals and academics. These connections can provide guidance, mentorship, and a deeper understanding of where foundational knowledge can take you. Networking is a crucial aspect of building your knowledge base, as it opens up avenues for learning that are not available in textbooks.

The transition to advanced courses demands a firm grasp of key themes and theories introduced in initial classes. These concepts become the pillars upon which more complex ideas are explored. Without a strong foundation, understanding the nuances of advanced topics can be challenging. It's akin to trying to read a sequel without knowing the story that precedes it.

Technology, too, plays a pivotal role in expanding your foundational knowledge. The proficiency in essential software and tools for research, coupled with digital literacy for presentations, sets the stage for success in sophisticated, technology-driven criminal justice environments. Technological competence complements traditional academic skills, making your foundation robust and adaptable.

Finally, reflection on your learning journey is an integral part of building on foundational knowledge. Reflective practices enable you to assess your understanding critically, identify gaps in your knowledge, and devise strategies to address them. This ongoing self-assessment ensures that your foundation remains strong and capable of supporting advanced studies and professional endeavors in the criminal justice field.

In conclusion, building upon foundational knowledge in criminal justice is a multi-faceted endeavor that extends beyond the confines of textbook learning. It involves academic rigor, practical experience, and personal reflection to create a sturdy base for advanced studies. As you continue on this academic journey, remember that every piece of knowledge acquired is a brick in the edifice of your future career. Your success in the field depends not just on the information you gather, but on how well you integrate and apply these insights into a cohesive, comprehensive understanding of criminal justice.

Chapter 10: The Road to Graduation and Beyond

The culmination of your studies in criminal justice isn't just a degree; it's a doorway to new horizons, equipped with the knowledge and skills to make a tangible difference in the world. As you approach the latter stages of your college journey, the significance of planning your academic path becomes paramount. Crafting a roadmap for the remainder of your college years requires a delicate balance of strategic course selection and real-world experience, ensuring not only academic enrichment but also professional preparedness. The exploration of career options with a criminal justice degree unveils a spectrum of opportunities ranging from law enforcement and legal careers to roles within corrections and rehabilitation. Each path offers unique challenges and rewards, singularly contributing to the vast mosaic of the criminal justice system. Furthermore, for those drawn to the pursuit of knowledge, graduate studies in criminal justice present an avenue for deeper exploration and specialization. Engaging in advanced study can open doors to academic positions, advanced research roles, and policy-making positions, further enabling you to contribute to the evolution of the field. As you navigate this journey, remember that the road to graduation is more than a quest for a diploma; it's a preparation for a lifetime commitment to justice, societal well-being, and continuous personal and professional growth.

Planning Your Academic Path

Navigating the path through your criminal justice education requires a blend of careful planning, determination, and an enthusiasm for the field that both challenges and rewards in equal measure. Like a well-woven tapestry, each thread in your academic experience contributes to the strength and texture of your eventual career tapestry. It's vital to consider not just the courses you select but how those courses align with your career aspirations and personal growth.

Your journey begins with an understanding that the criminal justice system is vast, touching upon aspects of law enforcement, legal practices, and corrections. This myriad of opportunities means that tailoring your academic path requires a strategic mindset. It's not simply a matter of picking and choosing classes at random but selecting those that will build upon each other, enhancing your understanding and skills in areas that interest you most.

Mapping out your academic journey should ideally start in your freshman year. This stage is critical, not only for setting the tone of your college experience but for laying down a solid foundation upon which to build. Introduction courses are more than just a checkbox on your degree plan; they open the doors to understanding the complex inter-workings of the criminal justice system. These foundational classes should be approached with the seriousness they deserve, providing the scaffolding needed for more specialized courses down the line.

As you progress, it becomes increasingly important to engage deeply with your courses. This isn't just about attending lectures and taking notes. It's about actively participating, asking questions, and connecting with your professors. These academic relationships can be pivotal, offering insights into the field, and potentially opening doors to opportunities like internships and research projects.

Speaking of internships, taking advantage of these experiences is a crucial aspect of your academic path. Internships provide a glimpse into the day-to-day operations of the criminal justice system, allowing you to apply theoretical knowledge in practical settings. They also serve as a valuable networking tool, connecting you with professionals in the field.

Another critical aspect of your academic planning is the capstone project or thesis required by many criminal justice programs in the final year. This project offers a chance to dive deep into a topic that fascinates you, under the guidance of a faculty advisor. It's an opportunity to demonstrate your understanding, analytical skills, and ability to conduct research. Choosing a topic that aligns with your career goals can make this project not just a graduation requirement but a launching pad for your career.

While focusing on your major, don't overlook the importance of general education courses. These classes, often seen as hurdles to get over, can enrich your understanding of the world and sharpen skills that are crucial in the criminal justice field, such as critical thinking, writing, and ethical reasoning.

Advancing through your program, it's essential to consider the balance between elective and required courses. Electives allow you to explore interests that might not be covered in your core curriculum, offering a broader educational experience. This is where you can tailor your education to fit your unique career ambitions, whether that's delving deeper into forensic psychology, juvenile justice, or cybercrime.

As graduation approaches, the question of what comes next looms large. For many, graduate school is the next step, offering an opportunity to specialize further in their chosen field. Researching potential graduate programs early can help you tailor your remaining undergraduate coursework to meet any prerequisites, making for a smoother transition to postgraduate study.

Ultimately, the key to success in planning your academic path is flexibility. The field of criminal justice is constantly evolving, with new challenges and areas of study emerging regularly. Staying informed about developments in the field will allow you to adjust your academic plan as necessary, ensuring that your education remains relevant and aligned with your goals.

In conclusion, the journey through your criminal justice education is one that you have the power to design. By approaching your academic planning with a strategic mindset, seeking out opportunities for hands-on learning, and forging connections within the field, you can lay a strong foundation for a fulfilling career in criminal justice. Remember, the choices you make today shape the opportunities available to you tomorrow. With dedication and purpose, your academic journey can open doors to a world of possibilities in the vast field of criminal justice.

Career Options with a Criminal Justice Degree

The culmination of your criminal justice studies isn't merely a ceremonial walk across the stage to receive your diploma; it's the gateway to a myriad of career paths that await beyond academia. Grounded in the scientific study of criminal behavior, law enforcement, and the legal system, a criminal justice degree offers a diverse platform from which graduates can embark on professionally rewarding and personally fulfilling careers. Whether your passion lies in the on-the-ground action of law enforcement, the strategic complexities of legal and court systems, or the rehabilitative processes within corrections, the skills, and knowledge you've honed throughout your academic journey are directly transferable to real-world settings. Graduates are not limited to traditional roles; the evolving nature of crime, fueled by technological advancements, calls for modern roles in cyber security and digital forensics, highlighting the degree's versatility. With a solid foundation in critical thinking, ethical decision-making, and effective communication, your criminal justice degree serves as your passport into a sector where the demand for educated professionals continues to rise, offering stability, growth, and the opportunity to make a tangible impact on society.

Law Enforcement Careers

Pursuing a career in law enforcement stands as one of the most dynamic and impactful paths within the criminal justice system. For those drawn to the frontline of public service, law enforcement offers a range of professions that are crucial to maintaining social order and public safety. This chapter delves into the multifaceted nature of law enforcement careers, equipping you, a freshman in college, with the knowledge to navigate and succeed in this field.

The cornerstone of law enforcement lies in its commitment to protect and serve. This mission permeates through various roles, from patrol officers to detectives, and extends into specialized units such as cybercrime and canine handlers. Each position requires a set of skills and attributes that are honed through both academic learning and practical experience.

At the core of a successful law enforcement career is a solid educational foundation. A degree in criminal justice not only provides the theoretical knowledge necessary for understanding the complexities of the law but also equips students with critical thinking and problem-solving skills essential for the field. Colleges and universities offer courses that cover a broad range of topics, including criminology, ethics, community policing, and investigative techniques.

Internships play a pivotal role in bridging the gap between academic learning and real-world applications. Engaging in internships with local law enforcement agencies or federal bodies introduces students to the practical aspects of the job. It's an opportunity to gain hands-on experience, which is invaluable when entering the workforce.

Networking within the law enforcement community can significantly benefit your career trajectory. Attending seminars, joining professional organizations, and connecting with mentors can open doors to opportunities and enrich your learning experience. Through these interactions, you gain insights into the varied facets of law enforcement and the latest trends and advancements in the field.

Technological proficiency has become increasingly crucial in law enforcement roles. Officers today must be adept at using advanced software for crime analysis, digital evidence retrieval, and information sharing. Academic courses that emphasize technology in criminal justice can provide a competitive edge in the job market.

Fostering strong communication skills is essential for law enforcement professionals. The ability to effectively interact with the public, disseminate information to colleagues, and articulate findings in written reports is fundamental. Coursework in communication, psychology, and sociology can enhance these skills, preparing you for the complexities of community interaction.

The ethical dimension of law enforcement can't be overstated. Professionals in this field face moral dilemmas and must make decisions that align with legal standards and community values. Ethics training is an integral part of the criminal justice curriculum, instilling a commitment to justice and integrity.

Leadership is another critical component of law enforcement careers. As you advance in your career, the ability to lead teams, manage resources, and develop strategic initiatives becomes imperative. Leadership courses and extracurricular activities such as ROTC or community service can foster these abilities.

Adaptability and resilience are traits that every law enforcement officer must possess. The unpredictable nature of the job requires individuals who can handle stress, think on their feet, and bounce back from challenging situations. Participating in stress management and resilience workshops can provide strategies for coping with the demands of the profession.

Physical fitness is also a requirement for most law enforcement positions. Agencies often have stringent fitness standards that candidates must meet. Engaging in regular physical training and adopting a healthy lifestyle can prepare you for the physical demands of the job.

Continuing education and specialization can further advance one's career in law enforcement. Growth opportunities include advanced degrees, specialized training programs, and certification in areas such as forensic investigation or cyber security. These endeavors not only enhance skills but also open up avenues for promotion and leadership roles.

The journey toward a career in law enforcement is both challenging and rewarding. It requires dedication, preparation, and a commitment to serving the community. By leveraging your education, embracing practical experiences, and continuously seeking professional development, you can achieve success and make a meaningful impact in the field of law enforcement.

In conclusion, law enforcement careers offer a dynamic and fulfilling path for those committed to public service. Through a combination of academic study, practical experience, and ongoing professional development, aspiring officers are well-equipped to meet the demands and opportunities of this vital field.

Legal and Court Careers In the world of criminal justice, the spotlight often shines most brightly on the dynamic and critical field of legal and court careers. These professions are not just pillars of the criminal justice system but are foundational to the very concept of justice itself. Embarking on a career within the legal and court system demands not only a solid educational grounding in the principles of criminal justice but also a deep commitment to the values of fairness, integrity, and the rule of law.

The realm of legal and court careers is vast and diverse, encompassing roles from judges and lawyers to court reporters and legal assistants. Each position plays a unique part in the intricate ballet of jurisprudence, where the stakes are nothing less than the balance of justice itself. For students of criminal justice, understanding these roles and the paths to achieving them can be the first step toward a fulfilling and impactful career.

Lawyers are perhaps the most recognizable figures in this domain, serving as the champions of legal battles, whether defending the accused or prosecuting in the name of the state. Their journey begins with a rigorous education path, first achieving a bachelor's degree before tackling law school and passing the bar exam. However, the preparation for this career starts even earlier, with courses in writing, public speaking, and ethics laying the groundwork for future success.

Judges, on the other hand, are the arbiters of the court, guiding proceedings with an impartial hand and ensuring that the law is applied fairly and consistently. Becoming a judge typically requires years of experience as a practicing lawyer and often, an appointment or election process. This role demands a deep understanding of the law, a firm ethical compass, and the capacity to make difficult decisions under pressure.

Beyond these visible roles, the legal system relies on a network of support staff to function. Court reporters, for instance, create the official record of court proceedings, a critical task requiring speed, accuracy, and meticulous attention to detail. Legal assistants and paralegals support lawyers and judges by managing case files, conducting research, and ensuring that the many pieces of the legal puzzle are in place.

For students interested in these careers, internships offer an invaluable glimpse into the legal world, providing hands-on experience and the opportunity to network with professionals in the field. Universities and colleges may provide connections to internships at law firms, courts, and government agencies, enabling students to apply their theoretical knowledge in real-world settings.

Additionally, moot court and mock trial competitions present students with the chance to develop and hone their legal skills in a competitive and supportive environment. These activities not only build confidence in public speaking and legal reasoning but also shine on a resume when seeking internships and employment post-graduation.

Educational requirements for legal and court careers vary widely by role but share a common thread: the need for continuous learning. The law is ever-evolving, and professionals in the field must stay abreast of changes to legislation and legal precedents. Pursuing a career in this sector means committing to ongoing education and professional development, whether through formal schooling, continuing legal education programs, or self-study.

The ethical considerations in legal and court careers cannot be overstated. Professionals in the justice system wield considerable power over individuals' lives and must adhere to the highest ethical standards. This includes a commitment to truth, fairness, and a responsibility to uphold the law above personal beliefs or ambitions.

Leadership skills are also crucial in legal and court careers. Lawyers, judges, and administrative staff must be able to lead teams, manage complex projects, and make tough decisions. Developing these skills during one's studies through group projects, leadership roles in clubs, and other activities can provide a firm foundation for future career success.

Digital literacy has become increasingly important in all facets of criminal justice, including legal and court careers. Familiarity with legal research databases, virtual court proceedings, and digital case management systems is becoming a standard expectation for new entrants into the field. Students should seize opportunities to develop these skills through courses, workshops, and hands-on experiences.

Networking is another critical element in building a career in the legal and court system. Engaging with professional organizations, attending seminars and workshops, and connecting with alumni can open doors to opportunities that might not be available otherwise. The value of a well-established professional network cannot be underestimated for anyone aspiring to a career in this challenging and rewarding field.

In conclusion, a career in legal and court systems offers the chance to make a significant impact on society. It's a career path characterized by challenges, lifelong learning, and the constant pursuit of justice. For those with a passion for upholding the rule of law and a dedication to serving their community, the legal and court system can provide a fulfilling and honorable career.

Students at the onset of their academic journey should be aware that success in this field requires more than just an understanding of legal principles. It demands resilience, ethical fortitude, and a commitment to continuous improvement. With these qualities, along with the practical skills and knowledge gained through education and experience, graduates can confidently navigate the path to meaningful and impactful careers in the legal and court systems.

Corrections and Rehabilitation Within the expansive domain of criminal justice, the concepts of corrections and rehabilitation stand as central pillars, embodying the resolve to transform individuals who have strayed, back onto a path of societal contribution. This chapter will delve deep into the nuances of corrections and rehabilitation, not merely from a punitive standpoint but as pivotal elements in fostering individual and societal change.

At the core of understanding corrections and rehabilitation is the recognition that human behavior can be modified, and lives reoriented towards constructive ends. This is not just an optimistic viewpoint; it's underpinned by rigorous academic and practical work in the fields of psychology, sociology, and criminology. The effectiveness of rehabilitation programs has been a subject of considerable research. For instance, studies have shown that carefully structured rehabilitation programs can significantly reduce reoffending rates, underscoring the potential for positive change (Lipsey et al., 2007).

Corrections embody a wide range of sanctions from incarceration to community-based sentences, all aimed at achieving a balance between punishing and rehabilitating offenders. The prison system, often viewed through a lens of retribution, also serves as a vessel for rehabilitative efforts. Educational programs, vocational training, therapy sessions, and drug rehabilitation efforts within correctional facilities are all geared toward equipping inmates with the skills and mindsets needed for reintegration into society.

Community-based rehabilitation takes a slightly different approach, emphasizing offender accountability while maintaining community ties. Programs such as probation, parole, and community service are designed not just to monitor and restrict but to support and guide. Through such programs, offenders receive a chance to make amends and gradually transition back into society, all while under the supervision of the criminal justice system.

The scientific investigation into the psychology of criminal behavior provides a foundation for many rehabilitation efforts. Understanding the factors that contribute to criminal behavior, including social, psychological, and economic factors, helps in crafting interventions that address these root causes directly (Andrews & Bonta, 2010).

Rehabilitation is not a one-size-fits-all solution; it requires a tailored approach that considers the unique circumstances and needs of each offender. This principle is critically important for young offenders, where the focus is on preventing the solidification of criminal habits and facilitating a return to a constructive role within society.

Technology plays a growing role in corrections and rehabilitation, from electronic monitoring that allows for restricted freedom to software programs designed to improve cognitive behavior. These technologies provide new avenues for rehabilitation that can be more flexible and responsive to individual needs.

However, challenges remain in the quest to balance societal safety with the rehabilitation of offenders. Overcrowding in prisons, limited resources for rehabilitation programs, and societal stigma against former offenders are persistent issues. Addressing these challenges requires a comprehensive approach that involves not just the criminal justice system, but also public policy, community initiatives, and societal attitudes towards redemption and second chances.

The role of education within corrections and rehabilitation cannot be overstated. Educational programs within prisons have been shown to reduce recidivism rates significantly. They offer a pathway for inmates to gain the skills and qualifications needed for employment post-release, thereby addressing one of the key triggers of reoffending – the lack of economic opportunity (Davis et al., 2014).

Rehabilitation also encompasses mental health treatment. The prevalence of mental health issues among prison populations is significantly higher than in the general population. Addressing these issues through comprehensive mental health services is crucial for the rehabilitation process, helping to mitigate one of the key factors contributing to criminal behavior.

The debate over the effectiveness of rehabilitation versus punishment is ongoing, with strong arguments on both sides. However, the evidence suggests that a balanced approach that incorporates elements of both strategies yields the most positive outcomes for offenders, victims, and society at large (MacKenzie, 2006).

Engaging with the community is a crucial aspect of the rehabilitation process. Community programs that support reintegration efforts can significantly reduce the barriers that former offenders face. These programs not only assist individuals in finding housing, employment, and continued education but also help in rebuilding familial and social connections.

The journey through corrections and rehabilitation is fraught with challenges and setbacks. Yet, it is a journey that reflects a fundamental belief in the possibility of change and redemption. It reinforces the idea that justice is not just about punishment but about fostering environments that encourage positive transformation.

In embarking on a study of the criminal justice system, it is essential to approach corrections and rehabilitation with an open mind. Recognizing the humanity in those who have erred and understanding the complex interplay of factors that contribute to criminal behavior is crucial. It is here, in the intersection of theory, practice, and compassion, that true progress lies.

As future professionals in the field of criminal justice, you are positioned to make significant contributions to this ongoing evolution. Whether through direct involvement in rehabilitation programs, policy formulation, or academic research, the opportunity to shape a more just and rehabilitative system awaits. It is a calling that demands not only intellectual acumen but a profound commitment to human dignity and the transformative power of second chances.

Graduate Studies in Criminal Justice

The journey through undergraduate studies in criminal justice is both a test and a testament to the dedication and passion for the field. For those who gaze further on the horizon, graduate studies in criminal justice open a new chapter filled with possibilities, deeper knowledge, and specialized skills. This path isn't merely a continuation of undergraduate work; it is a conscious step towards becoming a leader, an innovator, and a pivotal member of the criminal justice community.

Embarking on graduate studies is akin to embarking on a rigorous adventure that tests one's mettle, intellect, and ambition. It's a venture where critical thinking is honed to a fine edge, and the ability to question and challenge the status quo becomes second nature. The landscape of criminal justice is ever-evolving, and graduate studies prepare scholars for the forefront of change and innovation in this dynamic field.

Choosing the right program is the first critical step in this journey. This decision can't be made lightly. Prospective students must consider various factors, including the program's focus, faculty expertise, available resources, and how these align with their career aspirations. Each program offers a unique lens through which to view the criminal justice system, offering specializations ranging from criminology, law enforcement, and corrections, to forensic psychology.

The application process itself is a rigorous undertaking, requiring exceptional academic records, letters of recommendation, and often a statement of purpose that reflects the candidate's passion and readiness for advanced study. This phase is an opportunity to reflect on personal goals and how a graduate degree in criminal justice can pave the way to achieving them.

Once admitted, the curriculum in graduate programs tends to be intense, offering both breadth and depth in topics relevant to criminal justice. Students engage with advanced theories, contemporary research methodologies, and practical applications. Courses are designed to challenge students to think critically, analyze complex problems, and develop comprehensive solutions.

Research plays a pivotal role in graduate studies. It's through research that students contribute to the field, pushing the boundaries of current knowledge and practice. Whether it's through a thesis or a capstone project, graduate students have the opportunity to explore issues of interest deeply, under the guidance of experienced faculty members. This is where theory meets praxis, and students transform into scholars.

Internships and practical experiences are also integral to graduate studies, providing students with the chance to apply their knowledge in real-world settings. These experiences are invaluable, offering insights into the workings of the criminal justice system and helping to form professional connections that can be pivotal in one's career.

Networking and mentorship are crucial throughout the journey in graduate studies. Building relationships with faculty, peers, and professionals in the field opens the door to knowledge exchange, collaborations, and future job opportunities. It's through these interactions that students find guidance, inspiration, and the support necessary to navigate the challenges of graduate school.

The skillset acquired through graduate studies in criminal justice is vast and versatile, equipping students with the ability to analyze data, understand complex societal issues, and propose evidence-based solutions. These skills are not only applicable to careers within the criminal justice system but are also valuable in policy development, research, and academia.

Upon completion of a graduate program, the career paths available to graduates are both diverse and rewarding. Some may choose to pursue roles in federal or state law enforcement agencies, while others may find their calling in academia or policy analysis. The careers pursued post-graduation are a reflection of the broad applicability of a graduate degree in criminal justice, highlighting the versatility and importance of the field.

Students need to remain aware of the evolving nature of the criminal justice system and the broader societal implications of their work. The commitment to continuous learning and adaptation is what distinguishes great criminal justice professionals from good ones. Graduate studies provide a foundation, but the learning journey extends far beyond graduation.

For those contemplating graduate studies in criminal justice, the path is challenging but immensely rewarding. It is a commitment to personal and professional growth, and to contributing to a field that shapes the fabric of society. The road to graduation and beyond is paved with challenges, triumphs, and countless opportunities to make a meaningful impact.

In conclusion, graduate studies in criminal justice offer an enriching and comprehensive experience for those looking to delve deeper into the field. It's an investment in one's future, in the pursuit of justice, and in the betterment of society. As future leaders, scholars, and practitioners, graduate students in criminal justice are poised to make significant contributions to the field, armed with knowledge, skills, and a vision for a more just world.

Chapter 11: Professional Skills for the Criminal Justice Field

In the ever-evolving landscape of the criminal justice system, possessing a robust set of professional skills is not just an advantage—it's a necessity. As students step into this dynamic field, they must arm themselves with more than just theoretical knowledge. Communication, ethical decision-making, and leadership are pillars upon which a successful career in criminal justice is built. Effective communication skills are crucial for law enforcement officers, attorneys, and other professionals who interact with diverse populations and colleagues daily. These skills ensure a clear, concise exchange of information, critical in high-stakes environments where misunderstandings can have dire consequences. Ethical considerations and decision-making in criminal justice go beyond mere compliance with laws and regulations. They require a deep understanding of moral principles and the courage to make the right choices, even when faced with challenges. Leadership, on the other hand, is about inspiring and guiding others toward achieving common goals, an essential trait for those aspiring to roles of responsibility in this field. Building these competencies involves continuous learning and application, setting the foundation for not only career advancement but also for contributing to the justice system in a meaningful way.

Communication Skills

In the realm of criminal justice, clear and effective communication stands as one of the most invaluable skills you can cultivate. Whether it's deciphering the nuances of a complex case, negotiating during a high-stakes situation, or simply presenting evidence in a manner that's both cogent and compelling, the art of communication is indispensable. This chapter is dedicated to unraveling the layers of communication skills essential for anyone aspiring to excel in the criminal justice field.

The first cornerstone of excellent communication is active listening. In law enforcement, courtrooms, or corrections, the ability to listen can be just as critical as the ability to speak. Active listening involves fully concentrating on what is being said rather than just passively 'hearing' the message of the speaker. It's about understanding the message, asking clarifying questions, and responding appropriately (Jahromi et al, 2016). Practicing active listening enhances your ability to comprehend complex legal arguments, empathize with victims, and decipher subtleties in testimonies or negotiations.

Another critical facet of communication in criminal justice is verbal articulation. The ability to convey information in a clear, concise, and persuasive manner can significantly impact the outcome of a case. Whether you're giving testimony, briefing a team, or explaining rights to an individual being detained, the clarity of your verbal communication can make a substantial difference. Precision in language helps reduce misunderstandings and increases the effectiveness of your message.

Written communication also occupies a pivotal role in the criminal justice system. Reports, proposals, affidavits, and research papers form the backbone of documentation and evidence in many contexts. Mastery of written communication means being able to present information in a structured, logical, and professional manner. It's not just about what you're saying but how you're saying it; your written documents should be able to stand up to scrutiny in both academia and professional practice.

Non-verbal communication, though often overlooked, can be just as crucial as verbal and written modes. Body language, eye contact, and even the physical distance between communicators can convey a wealth of information. In interviews, interrogations, and interactions with peers, being aware of and controlling your non-verbal cues can enhance the effectiveness of your communication.

Fostering cultural competency is another significant aspect. The criminal justice system intersects with individuals from diverse backgrounds, each with its own set of values, beliefs, and modes of communication. Cultivating an understanding and respect for this diversity can improve interactions and operations within communities. Cultural competency not only enriches your professional skill set but also aligns with ethical practices in criminal justice.

The digital age has also ushered in the importance of digital literacy in communication. Effective use of technology to convey and receive messages, whether through email, social media, or other digital platforms, has become essential. Navigating these digital landscapes with discretion and professionalism is a modern-day communication skill that's rapidly gaining importance.

Clarifying complex ideas for various audiences is a skill that cannot be overstated. Whether it's translating legal jargon for the layman, crafting policy proposals for stakeholders, or teaching criminal justice concepts to students, the ability to distill complex information into understandable pieces is invaluable.

Ethical communication is a cornerstone of criminal justice. Every word spoken or written carries the weight of ethical consideration. It's about being honest, transparent, and respectful, irrespective of the scenario. Upholding ethical standards in all forms of communication reinforces the credibility and integrity of the criminal justice system as a whole.

Conflict resolution skills are also tied deeply with effective communication. In many situations, criminal justice professionals find themselves mediating disputes or de-escalating contentious situations. The ability to navigate these conflicts with diplomacy and tact relies heavily on your communication prowess.

Persuasion and negotiation are skills that, when mastered, can significantly impact your career in criminal justice. Whether it's persuading a jury, negotiating during a hostage situation, or convincing stakeholders to support a policy change, the power of persuasion is a formidable tool in your arsenal.

Feedback, both giving and receiving, is an essential communication skill. Constructive feedback can foster professional growth and development, while the ability to receive and act on feedback demonstrates openness and adaptability. These traits are incredibly valuable in the ever-evolving field of criminal justice.

Finally, the ability to communicate under pressure is a trait that sets apart competent criminal justice professionals. High-stress situations are commonplace in this field, from courtroom proceedings to crisis negotiations. Staying calm and maintaining clear, effective communication in these scenarios can be the difference between resolution and escalation.

As you embark on your journey through the criminal justice system, consider the development of your communication skills as a lifelong pursuit. The effectiveness of your professional practice in criminal justice is inextricably linked to your ability to communicate, ethically, and effectively. Embrace every opportunity to listen, speak, write, and engage with others. The mastery of communication will serve as a foundation upon which you can build a successful and fulfilling career.

Ethical Considerations and Decision-Making

In the realm of criminal justice, the weight of our decisions can often be monumental, carrying with them the potential to significantly alter lives and shape societal norms. As we delve into the landscape of ethical decision-making within this field, it's crucial to understand that these decisions are not simply black and white but exist within vast shades of grey. The underpinning of our ethical landscape is grounded in a commitment to justice, fairness, and the unwavering respect for individual rights.

The cornerstone of ethical decision-making in criminal justice revolves around the principles of justice and equity. Professionals within this sphere are consistently faced with situations that require a meticulous balance between the letter of the law and the spirit of fairness. This balancing act ensures that the application of laws does not disproportionately affect one group more than another, thereby maintaining a foundation of equity.

At its core, ethical decision-making necessitates an in-depth understanding of moral philosophy and the ethical theories that have shaped our current perspectives on justice. The dilemmas faced by law enforcement officers, judges, and correctional officers are often complex, requiring a nuanced understanding of ethical principles such as utilitarianism, deontology, and the ethics of care (Arrigo, 2014). These theories provide a framework through which professionals can navigate the moral complexities of their roles, striving always to act in a manner that promotes the greatest good while upholding individual rights and dignity.

One pivotal aspect of ethical decision-making in criminal justice is the adherence to the principle of integrity. This principle obliges professionals to act with honesty and virtue, ensuring that their actions are consistent with moral and ethical standards. Integrity is the bedrock upon which public trust is built, and without it, the very foundation of our legal system begins to crumble (Pollock, 2013).

Moreover, the ethical considerations in criminal justice extend beyond the individual level to encompass organizational ethics. The culture of a law enforcement agency, court system, or correctional facility heavily influences the ethical behavior of its members. Creating an environment that encourages ethical decision-making and holds individuals accountable for their actions is paramount. This involves not only the establishment of clear ethical guidelines but also the provision of ongoing ethical training and education to ensure these standards are deeply ingrained (Banks, 2016).

Furthermore, the application of ethical decision-making in the criminal justice system is continually challenged by rapidly evolving societal norms and technology. Issues such as digital privacy, cybercrime, and the use of artificial intelligence in policing require a reevaluation of traditional ethical frameworks. Professionals must be adept at foreseeing potential ethical dilemmas that may arise from these advancements and prepared to address them with foresight and wisdom.

Transparency and accountability are also critical components of ethical decision-making in criminal justice. These values foster trust between the criminal justice system and the communities they serve. It is essential, therefore, that criminal justice professionals are not only held to high ethical standards but are also willing to be held accountable for their actions in a transparent manner. This fosters a culture of responsibility and community engagement, crucial for the effective functioning of the justice system.

Another consideration is the challenge of personal biases and prejudices. Ethical decision-making requires a high level of self-awareness and the ability to recognize and mitigate personal biases that may influence decision-making processes. This is particularly important in a field that is as diverse and multifaceted as criminal justice, where decisions can significantly impact individuals from varied backgrounds and walks of life.

The role of empathy in ethical decision-making cannot be overstated. It is the ability to understand and share the feelings of another that often guides criminal justice professionals toward more compassionate and fair decisions. In a field often criticized for its harshness, a dose of empathy can be the key to ensuring justice is served in a manner that is both effective and humane.

Education and continuous learning play a significant role in enhancing ethical decision-making capabilities. As fresh minds enter the field, armed with the latest in ethical theory and practice, they bring with them the opportunity to challenge the status quo and elevate the standard of ethical conduct within the criminal justice system.

It is also worth noting the impact of leadership on ethical decision-making. Leaders within criminal justice organizations wield significant influence over the behavior and decision-making of their subordinates. Hence, ethical leadership not only involves making ethical decisions oneself but also inspiring others to do the same, thereby cultivating an environment where ethical considerations are at the forefront of decision-making processes.

In conclusion, the journey through the landscape of ethical considerations and decision-making in the criminal justice field is both challenging and rewarding. It is a path paved with complex dilemmas, philosophical debates, and the constant pursuit of justice. However, it is also a journey that allows individuals to make a profound impact on society, upholding the principles of fairness, dignity, and equity. As we continue to confront and navigate these ethical challenges, we do so with the knowledge that our choices shape not only the lives of individuals but the fabric of society itself.

Leadership in Criminal Justice

Leadership within the realm of criminal justice isn't merely a position or a title; it's an active, ongoing process that involves critical thinking, ethical decision-making, and the ability to inspire and guide others toward achieving shared objectives. It's about making tough decisions under pressure, resolving conflicts, and steering both individuals and teams toward a common goal. As you embark on your journey to understand and eventually master the art of leadership in this field, remember that the most effective leaders are those who lead by example, are committed to their cause, and understand the importance of integrity and accountability.

The landscape of criminal justice is complex and ever-evolving, requiring leaders who are not only well-versed in the current laws and procedures but also capable of adapting to change. This necessity for adaptability is compounded by the unpredictable nature of crime and the constant technological advancements that both aid and challenge the field. Leaders in criminal justice must therefore be lifelong learners, always ready to update their knowledge and skills to stay ahead of the curve.

Communicating effectively is another cornerstone of strong leadership in criminal justice. Leaders must be able to convey their ideas clearly, listen actively, and resolve misunderstandings or conflicts promptly and efficiently. This involves not just verbal communication but also the ability to write clearly and persuasively, as well as to utilize various forms of digital communication. Whether addressing a team, speaking with the community, or presenting a case, effective communication skills are essential for success.

Another essential aspect of leadership in this field is ethical decision-making. Criminal justice leaders are often faced with situations that challenge their morals and require difficult choices to be made. It's here that the importance of having a strong ethical framework comes into play, guiding leaders to make decisions that are not only legally sound but also morally just. This can sometimes mean going against the grain or choosing the more challenging path because it's the right thing to do.

Teamwork and collaboration are also vital components of leadership in criminal justice. Leaders must be able to bring people together, fostering an environment of mutual respect and cooperation. This involves recognizing and valuing the diverse skills and perspectives that each team member brings to the table, and knowing how to blend these differences into a cohesive, effective unit. It's about building trust and respect, qualities that can significantly enhance a team's productivity and morale.

To become impactful leaders in criminal justice, students must engage in real-world experiences. This could mean participating in internships, volunteer programs, or any other form of experiential learning that offers a glimpse into the leadership roles within the field. Such experiences not only provide practical skills but also help in understanding the challenges and rewards of leadership positions.

Moreover, aspiring leaders should seek mentors who exemplify the qualities of effective leadership. Learning from experienced professionals can provide invaluable insights and guidance, helping to shape one's leadership style and approach. This mentorship, combined with academic learning, can significantly enrich a student's understanding and capability in leadership roles.

In addition to gaining practical experience and mentorship, engaging in continuous education is crucial. The criminal justice field is continually affected by new laws, technologies, and societal changes. Leaders must stay informed about these developments through ongoing education, whether it be formal coursework, seminars, workshops, or self-study. This commitment to learning demonstrates a leader's dedication to their role and their willingness to evolve and adapt.

Furthermore, developing resilience is key for leaders in criminal justice. They often face high-pressure situations, setbacks, and even failures. Resilience—the ability to bounce back from these challenges—is what allows leaders to learn from their experiences, maintain their commitment, and continue to inspire and guide their teams effectively.

It's also important for future leaders in criminal justice to understand the importance of inclusivity and diversity. Leaders should strive to create an environment where every voice is heard and valued, recognizing the strength that lies in diverse perspectives. This not only enriches the decision-making process but also contributes to a more equitable and just criminal justice system.

As you progress through your studies and eventually your career, remember that leadership is not something you're born with but a skill set that can be developed over time. It requires patience, effort, and a genuine desire to make a positive impact on the lives of others and the community at large. With the right mindset and dedication, anyone can become an effective leader in the criminal justice field.

In conclusion, leadership in criminal justice is multi-faceted and demands a deep understanding of the law, excellent communication skills, ethical integrity, and the ability to lead and inspire others. It's a lifelong journey of learning, adaptation, and commitment to serving justice. By focusing on developing these essential skills and qualities, students can prepare themselves for successful and fulfilling careers as future leaders in the criminal justice system.

Chapter 12: Global Perspectives on Criminal Justice

In this rapidly globalizing world, understanding criminal justice from a global perspective is imperative for anyone studying in this field. This chapter delves into how different countries approach criminal justice, exploring the diversity and complexity of systems worldwide. We'll uncover the nuances of international criminal justice systems, emphasizing comparisons that highlight the unique blend of cultural, social, and legal factors shaping each system (Reichel, 2013). As the forces of globalization draw societies closer, the impact of transcending borders is profound, not just economically but in the realms of crime and justice as well. Issues such as human trafficking, cybercrime, and international terrorism necessitate a collaborative and informed response from the global community. This chapter aims to equip you with a broader understanding, encouraging you to think critically about the interconnectedness of criminal justice practices around the world. By embracing a global perspective, you'll be better prepared to address challenges and contribute effectively to discussions on international crime and justice (Natarajan, 2011; Shelley, 2018).

Comparing International Criminal Justice Systems

As we delve deeper into the realm of criminal justice from a global standpoint, it becomes increasingly important to understand how different nations approach the concept of justice and law enforcement. The criminal justice systems around the world are as varied as the cultures from which they originate. This chapter aims to shed light on these differences, highlighting the importance of a broad perspective when studying criminal justice.

The United States, for instance, operates under a dual system of federal and state laws, which can sometimes lead to complexities and inconsistencies. In contrast, countries like the United Kingdom rely on a single legal system that applies to all territories within the kingdom, offering a more uniform application of justice. This notable difference not only impacts the legislative process but also influences the enforcement and administration of the law.

Another aspect worth examining is the approach to corrections and rehabilitation. Scandinavian countries like Norway embody the philosophy of restorative justice, focusing on rehabilitating rather than punishing offenders. The Norwegian criminal justice system prioritizes the social reintegration of prisoners, evident in its low recidivism rates, compared to countries with more punitive approaches (Jensen & Petersen, 2019). This stark contrast offers valuable insights into the effectiveness of rehabilitation over retribution.

Furthermore, the role of law enforcement varies significantly across borders. In Japan, for instance, community policing plays a central role in maintaining public safety, with officers often engaging in daily life activities within communities to build trust and deter crime proactively (Takagi & Kawachi, 2021). This approach contrasts with more militarized policing strategies seen in other nations, underscoring the importance of cultural context in shaping law enforcement practices.

The judicial processes also differ widely. Inquisitorial systems, used in countries like France and Germany, involve a more active role for judges, who participate in the investigation process. This system is quite different from the adversarial system prevalent in the Anglo-American legal tradition, where two parties advocate before a neutral judge or jury (Jones, 2021). Each system has its merits and challenges, influencing the efficiency and fairness of legal proceedings.

Penalties and sentencing provide another area of stark contrast. The use of capital punishment varies widely, with some countries having abolished it entirely, while others, like the United States and China, still implement it under specific circumstances. This divergence points to fundamental differences in societal attitudes towards justice and the value of human life.

Digital innovation and cybersecurity have also become critical factors in the criminal justice landscape. Nations like Estonia have pioneered the integration of digital technology into their legal and administrative processes, enhancing efficiency and accessibility. Conversely, countries lagging in digital adoption face challenges in managing cybercrime and ensuring justice in the digital age.

In exploring these international criminal justice systems, it's crucial to recognize the societal, cultural, and historical contexts that shape them. The concept of justice is not a one-size-fits-all model. Each country's system reflects its unique values, challenges, and history, offering invaluable lessons on the variety of ways to approach law and order.

Studying these international differences enriches our understanding by providing a broader spectrum of perspectives on what justice can look like. It reminds us that there are multiple ways to achieve a just society, each with its strengths and weaknesses. For criminal justice students, this global perspective is not just an academic exercise; it's a vital lens through which to assess and appreciate the complexity of justice.

As we look towards the future, the criminal justice field must continue to evolve and adapt, drawing on these international experiences and innovations. The globalization of crime, especially cybercrime, demands a more cohesive and cooperative international approach to criminal justice. Just as crime crosses borders, so too must our efforts to understand and combat it.

Finally, for those embarking on a journey into criminal justice studies, remember that the heart of this field lies in its quest for fairness, equity, and a safer society for all. The diversity of international criminal justice systems offers a rich tapestry of strategies and philosophies. Embracing this diversity can inspire new solutions to age-old challenges, pushing the boundaries of what is possible in the pursuit of justice.

By comparing and learning from the myriad of criminal justice systems around the world, students and professionals alike can contribute to a more just and understanding global community. Let the exploration of these systems inspire you to think creatively and critically about how justice is administered both at home and abroad. The journey through the landscape of international criminal justice is both challenging and rewarding, filled with lessons that extend far beyond the classroom.

The Impact of Globalization on Criminal Justice

In an era where the world has become increasingly interconnected, the implications of globalization on criminal justice systems worldwide are profound and multifaceted. The phenomenon of globalization influences laws, crime patterns, law enforcement practices, judicial processes, and correctional systems, shaping them in ways that necessitate a broadened understanding beyond local or national perspectives.

One visible impact of globalization is the rise in transnational crime. Criminal networks have expanded their operations beyond borders, engaging in drug trafficking, human trafficking, cybercrime, and terrorism. These crimes challenge local law enforcement agencies, which often find themselves ill-equipped to handle crimes that originate beyond their jurisdiction. The necessity for international cooperation and coordination among law enforcement agencies has never been more critical.

Moreover, the globalization of crime brings to the fore the issue of legal jurisdiction. As crimes transcend borders, determining which nation's laws are applicable and how suspects are to be prosecuted and extradited becomes complex. This complexity necessitates legal frameworks that accommodate the transnational nature of these crimes, requiring countries to revise existing laws and engage in international legal cooperation.

Globalization also impacts criminal justice through the spread of ideas and standards concerning human rights and the rule of law. International norms and agreements, like the United Nations conventions against corruption and transnational organized crime, set standards that influence national criminal justice policies and practices. These international benchmarks push countries towards reform, aiming to improve fairness, efficiency, and integrity within criminal justice systems.

Additionally, the digital revolution, a key component of globalization, has drastically altered the landscape of crime and criminal investigation. Cybercrime, unknown a few generations ago, now poses one of the most significant global threats. This new crime frontier requires law enforcement and criminal justice professionals to acquire new skills and knowledge in cybersecurity and digital forensics.

On the flip side, globalization offers opportunities for sharing best practices and innovations in criminal justice among nations. Through international conferences, workshops, and collaborative research, professionals across the globe can learn from each other's experiences, adopting strategies that have been successful elsewhere. This exchange promotes a more unified global response to crime and justice.

Another aspect of globalization is the influence of migration patterns on criminal justice systems. As people move across borders, they bring with them diverse cultural and legal expectations. This diversity can lead to friction and misunderstandings within local legal systems, highlighting the need for cultural competence among criminal justice professionals. Understanding and respecting the cultural backgrounds of individuals in the system can improve community relations and enhance the effectiveness of justice delivery.

Regarding corrections, globalization has instigated a debate on prison practices and the treatment of offenders. The dissemination of information on correctional strategies and outcomes allows for the comparison and critique of prison systems globally. This scrutiny has led to calls for reforms, with an emphasis on rehabilitation over punishment, influenced by practices in countries that have successfully implemented such strategies.

However, the impact of globalization is not uniformly positive. The harmonization of criminal justice practices across different legal systems raises concerns about the erosion of national sovereignty and the dilution of local customs and traditions. Furthermore, the emphasis on international standards may overlook the unique social, economic, and cultural contexts of each country, potentially leading to policies and practices that are ineffective or inappropriate in specific settings.

Globalization also exacerbates inequalities within criminal justice systems. Wealthier nations often have more resources to adapt to the changes brought about by globalization, while poorer countries may struggle, leading to disparities in the effectiveness of crime prevention and justice delivery.

To navigate the complexities introduced by globalization, education, and training in criminal justice must evolve. It is essential to incorporate global perspectives into curricula, preparing students to operate in an international context. Understanding global crime trends, international law, and comparative criminal justice systems is crucial for the next generation of criminal justice professionals.

Strategic international partnerships and collaborative efforts can enhance capacity-building in less-developed criminal justice systems. Such collaborations can include the sharing of technology, expertise, and resources, aiming to elevate global standards of justice and law enforcement.

In conclusion, the impact of globalization on criminal justice is intricate, presenting challenges that require cooperative, innovative, and informed responses. As criminal justice practitioners and policymakers navigate these challenges, the goal should remain clear: to foster a world where justice is accessible, equitable, and effective, transcending borders to protect and serve the global community.

Embracing the complexities of globalization in criminal justice is not merely an academic exercise but a practical necessity. As the world continues to shrink through technological advances and increased connectivity, the criminal justice field must adapt, ensuring it is prepared to address not only today's challenges but also those of the future. Through education, collaboration, and a commitment to universal human rights, the global criminal justice community can strive towards a more just and secure world.

Embarking on Your Criminal Justice Journey

As you stand on the precipice of this monumental journey into the world of criminal justice, it's important to recognize the path you've chosen is both noble and challenging. The realm of criminal justice is vast, encompassing law enforcement, court systems, and corrections, each with its intricacies and nuances. This book has endeavored to lay the foundational stones upon which you will build your academic and professional career. Now, as we transition from the theoretical groundwork to the practical steps ahead, it's vital to reflect on the journey you are about to undertake.

The first step in this journey requires a deep understanding of the major components of the criminal justice system. Knowledge of how law enforcement, court systems, and corrections operate and interlink is crucial. However, it's the interdisciplinary approach that will truly enable you to grasp the complexities of this field. It's about connecting dots from seemingly disparate disciplines to create a comprehensive understanding of criminal justice (Jones et al., 2020).

Diving into your first year, the establishment of robust study habits and effective time management skills will be imperative. The world of criminal justice is as demanding as it is rewarding, and your success will largely hinge on your ability to engage deeply with your courses and manage your time efficiently. This will not only prepare you for the complexities of the subject matter but will also instill a discipline that will benefit you throughout your career.

The general education requirements, while at times may seem unrelated to your major, are complementary. They offer perspectives and skills that are invaluable to a well-rounded criminal justice professional. Whether it's developing critical thinking skills or understanding societal contexts, these courses lay the groundwork for a holistic approach to your studies (Smith & Williams, 2021).

Leveraging university resources can significantly augment your learning experience. Libraries and online databases offer a wealth of knowledge that can deepen your understanding of criminal justice. Additionally, utilizing the writing center and finding a tutor can enhance your research and writing skills, which are indispensable in this field.

Proper citation and adherence to APA formatting is not just academic rigor—it's a discipline that reflects the precision and attention to detail required in criminal justice. Mastering APA style will not only assist you in your academic endeavors but also prepare you for professional writing and reporting in your future career.

Excellence in writing within the criminal justice domain cannot be overstated. It requires a meticulous approach to research, an ability to craft cogent arguments, and a commitment to revising and refining your work. These skills are fundamental, whether you are drafting a policy proposal, a legal brief, or a report on criminal trends.

Engaging in experiential learning through internships, volunteer opportunities, and networking can provide invaluable real-world experience. These experiences not only enrich your understanding of criminal justice but also offer opportunities to connect with professionals in the field, opening doors to future career opportunities.

The advent of technology has transformed the landscape of criminal justice studies. Familiarity with essential software, tools, and digital literacy for research and presentations will enhance your efficacy as a student and as a professional in this ever-evolving field.

As you prepare for advanced courses, building on the foundational knowledge acquired in your initial years will be key. Understanding key themes and theories in criminal justice will enable you to analyze complex issues and contribute meaningful insights to discussions and solutions within the field.

The journey towards graduation and beyond is a journey of continuous learning and professional development. Planning your academic path with an eye on career options in law enforcement, legal and court careers, corrections, and rehabilitation, or even graduate studies, requires foresight and strategic planning.

Developing professional skills, particularly in communication, ethical considerations, and leadership, will distinguish you in the field of criminal justice. These skills are critical in navigating the challenges and responsibilities that come with a career in this domain.

Furthermore, a global perspective on criminal justice will enhance your understanding of the international dimensions of law, crime, and justice. It prepares you for the impact of globalization on criminal justice policies and practices, equipping you to address issues from a broader perspective.

In conclusion, as you embark on your criminal justice journey, remember that it's a path filled with challenges, opportunities, and profound responsibilities. The knowledge and skills you've begun to develop through your academic journey are the tools you will use to navigate this complex field. Stay curious, remain committed, and always strive for excellence. The journey may be long, but it is undoubtedly rewarding, and it's a journey that matters—not just for you, but for the society you will serve.

Appendix A: Appendix

As you transition from the main content of this guide into the appendices, it's essential to recognize the importance of supplementary resources in your academic journey. The appendices are designed not just as an afterthought, but as a crucial toolbox to enhance your understanding and application of the criminal justice system studies. Appendix A, in particular, offers a compilation of resources that are invaluable to your success both in and out of the classroom.

APA Quick Reference Guide

One of the first tools in this appendix is the APA Quick Reference Guide. Adhering to APA formatting and citation standards is fundamental in criminal justice studies, ensuring that your work maintains professional and scholarly integrity. This guide simplifies the complexity of APA rules, making it accessible for you to correctly cite your sources and format your academic papers. It provides clear examples of in-text citations, reference lists, and paper formatting to help you avoid common pitfalls and mistakes. Remember, precise citation not only respects the intellectual property of others but also strengthens the credibility of your work (American Psychological Association, 2020).

Criminal Justice Professional Organizations and Resources

Beyond the classroom, engaging with the broader criminal justice community is pivotal. This section introduces you to a range of professional organizations and resources that can provide insights into current trends, ongoing research, and networking opportunities. For instance, joining the American Society of Criminology can connect you with experts in the field and expose you to new perspectives and methodologies in criminal justice research (American Society of Criminology, n.d.). Similarly, the National Criminal Justice Association offers resources on policy development, funding opportunities, and legislative updates relevant to criminal justice professionals (National Criminal Justice Association, n.d.). Engaging with these organizations can significantly impact your academic and professional growth, offering a bridge between theoretical knowledge and real-world application.

In stepping into the realm of criminal justice, remember that your education is not just about acquiring knowledge but also about fostering connections and understanding the practical implications of that knowledge. Let this appendix serve as a starting point for you to explore, engage, and excel in your criminal justice studies.

APA Quick Reference Guide

Embarking on your journey through the criminal justice landscape in college, you'll soon find that the ability to articulate your findings and arguments with precision isn't just a necessity; it's an art. An essential component of this art, especially for freshmen such as yourself, is mastering the APA (American Psychological Association) formatting style. This quick reference guide intends to sharpen your skills in this area, laying a foundation that will support your academic and research efforts.

First up, let's talk about the basics. The APA style is not just about referencing sources correctly, though that's a significant part. It extends to the overall presentation of your work, including margins, font choices, and the inclusion of headers and page numbers. When you format your paper according to APA guidelines, you're not just following rules; you're ensuring that your work communicates clearly and effectively to your readers (American Psychological Association, 2020).

At the heart of APA formatting are the citations. Citations serve as the roadmap for your readers to follow the paths you've wandered through your research. When you cite sources within your text, known as in-text citations, the APA style prefers an author-date method. This minimalist approach allows your narrative to flow without interruption while still guiding your reader to the corresponding reference entry at the end of your work.

Creating a reference list is your next step. Each citation in your text needs a matching entry in your reference list, where full details of the source are provided. This allows your readers to seek out your sources, understand your influences, and appreciate the breadth of your research (American Psychological Association, 2020). Remember, your reference list is more than just a formality; it's an integral part of your academic discourse, enabling others to trace your steps through the intricate dance of scholarship.

When it comes to citing different types of works, the APA style is versatile yet precise. Whether you're citing a journal article, a book chapter, or a website, there are specific formats and rules to follow. For journal articles, the basic structure includes the author's name, publication year, article title, journal name, volume number, and page range. Books follow a similar pattern but are adapted for their form. For websites, the inclusion of a retrieval date has now been waived except for content that changes over time, such as social media profiles.

It's also worth noting the importance of digital sources in today's research context. With digital literacy becoming ever more critical, APA's latest edition accommodates the citing of online databases, social media, and even mobile apps. This flexibility underscores the evolving nature of research and the importance of staying current with how you collect and cite your sources (American Psychological Association, 2020).

Paraphrasing and quoting directly are two techniques you'll use to incorporate sources into your text. When paraphrasing, you're translating the essence of an idea into your own words, which requires a citation to credit the original author. Direct quotes, on the other hand, reproduce the source word for word and require a citation including the page number or paragraph number for non-paginated sources. These strategies allow you to weave others' ideas into your narrative seamlessly.

The APA style extends its precision to the presentation of numbers and statistics, an area of utmost importance for criminal justice majors. Whether you're presenting crime rates, survey results, or experimental data, how you report numbers—using numerals or words, formatting percentages, and tables—follows specific APA guidelines to ensure clarity and consistency (American Psychological Association, 2020).

Tables and figures are another crucial aspect of presenting information in your papers. APA formatting provides a framework for integrating tables and figures effectively, focusing on accessibility and comprehension for your readers. This includes labeling and citing each table and figure in the text, ensuring that your visual aids enhance, rather than confuse your narrative.

And let's not forget the fundamentals of paper formatting. Your essays and research papers should start with a title page, crafted according to APA specifications, that presents your paper's title, your name, and your institutional affiliation. Following this, an abstract summarizing your paper's key points may be required, depending on your assignment's guidelines.

Heading levels within APA style serve to structure your paper's content, making it easily navigable for readers. The use of headings organizes your arguments and research findings into a coherent flow, guiding readers through your exploration of the topic. It's not just about presenting information; it's about crafting a journey for your readers to follow.

When faced with the challenge of explaining complex legal or ethical issues within criminal justice topics, integrating direct quotes from statutes or precedent-setting cases lends authority to your arguments. APA style precise citing of legal materials ensures your arguments are supported by the foundational texts of your field.

In conclusion, embracing APA style isn't merely a curricular requirement; it's about joining a scholarly conversation with clear, structured, and accessible communication. As you delve deeper into your criminal justice studies, the proficiency you develop in APA formatting will not only elevate your academic work but also prepare you for the professional writing you'll undertake in your career.

A journey of a thousand miles begins with a single step, and mastering the APA format is a step towards scholarly excellence in your criminal justice education. As you progress, remember the importance of precision, integrity, and clarity in your academic endeavors. These qualities, reflected in your adherence to APA style, will serve you well throughout your college career and beyond.

Criminal Justice Professional Organizations and Resources

Embarking on a journey through the criminal justice system involves not only understanding the intricate components of law enforcement, courts, and corrections but also connecting with the broader community that shapes this dynamic field. For students forging their paths in criminal justice, tapping into the wealth of knowledge and networking opportunities presented by professional organizations is a critical step toward success. This section delves into the essential resources and professional organizations that serve as the backbone for aspiring criminal justice professionals.

Professional organizations in criminal justice offer a trove of benefits, including access to the latest research, industry trends, policy updates, and networking opportunities. These groups serve as a compass guiding members through the complexities of the criminal justice field, providing resources that are instrumental in both academic and professional development.

The American Society of Criminology (ASC) stands as a pillar in the criminal justice community, offering an interdisciplinary approach to understanding crime and delinquency. Membership in ASC is not just about adding a line to a resumé; it's about becoming part of a global network of professionals dedicated to the scientific study of crime. The society hosts annual meetings and publishes scholarly journals, such as *The Criminology Journal*, which serves as a crucial resource for staying abreast of new findings and theories.

Another vital resource for students is the Academy of Criminal Justice Sciences (ACJS). ACJS prides itself on promoting criminal justice education, research, and policy analysis within the discipline. Through its certification programs, comprehensive journals such as *Justice Quarterly*, and dynamic conferences, ACJS provides a broad platform for professional development and scholarly exchange.

For those with a keen interest in the practical application of criminal justice, the National Criminal Justice Association (NCJA) offers insights into policy development and implementation. NCJA's focus on promoting effective justice policies and practices makes it an indispensable resource for students aiming to influence public policy or pursue careers in governmental agencies.

In addition to these organizations, students should also consider special interest groups within the field, such as the International Association of Women Police (IAWP) and the National Organization of Black Law Enforcement Executives (NOBLE). These organizations offer unique perspectives and support for underrepresented voices in the criminal justice system, providing mentorship, scholarships, and advocacy on issues of diversity and inclusion.

Academic journals are another critical resource for criminal justice students. Publications like *The Journal of Criminal Justice* and *The Journal of Prison Education and Reentry* offer deep dives into specific areas of interest, presenting case studies, policy analysis, and research findings that enrich a student's understanding of complex issues.

Beyond journals and professional organizations, numerous online resources can supplement a criminal justice education. Websites such as the National Institute of Justice and the Bureau of Justice Statistics offer up-to-date data, research findings, and policy papers for free, enabling students to stay informed on current trends and data.

Networking events hosted by these organizations provide invaluable opportunities for students to connect with professionals, academics, and peers within the criminal justice field. Conferences, webinars, and workshops offer forums to engage with new ideas, discuss current challenges, and build relationships that can support career aspirations.

Mentorship programs available through these organizations can also offer guidance and support as students navigate their academic and professional journeys. Learning from experienced professionals provides insights into potential career paths, helps in developing professional skills, and sometimes even opens the door to job opportunities.

Finally, it's important for students to actively participate in these organizations and resources. Engagement can take many forms, from attending events and contributing to discussions to volunteering and serving on committees. Active participation not only enriches one's education but also strengthens the criminal justice community as a whole.

In conclusion, the path to success in the criminal justice field is paved with the knowledge, connections, and experiences gained through involvement in professional organizations and resources. Whether it's staying informed with the latest research, networking with seasoned professionals, or contributing to the discourse on important issues, these opportunities are invaluable for any student aspiring to make a difference in the realm of criminal justice.

Glossary of Key Terms

As we venture further into the study of criminal justice, it's crucial to grasp the foundational terms that will be a part of your academic and professional journey. This glossary serves as your beacon, illuminating key terms you'll encounter throughout your studies. It's designed not just to define but to inspire a deeper understanding of the criminal justice system's intricacies. Here, we distill complex concepts into accessible knowledge, marrying the rigorous demands of academia with the fervor of discovery and the drive for societal improvement.

1. Criminal Justice System

The network of government institutions and practices directed towards upholding social control, deterring and mitigating crime, and sanctioning those who violate laws with criminal penalties and rehabilitation efforts. The system is composed of three main components: law enforcement, the court system, and corrections.

2. Law Enforcement

Refers to the agencies and officers responsible for enforcing laws, maintaining public order, and providing services to prevent crime and its escalation. Law enforcement agencies include the police, sheriffs, and federal agencies such as the FBI and Homeland Security.

3. Court System

The judiciary arm of the criminal justice system where disputes are adjudicated, guilt or innocence is determined, and justice is dispensed. The court system spans from local courts handling misdemeanors to the Supreme Court resolving matters of constitutional law.

4. Corrections

This sector is responsible for enforcing the penalties determined by courts, including incarceration, probation, and parole. Corrections aims at rehabilitating offenders and preparing them for reintegration into society.

5. Interdisciplinary Approach

An approach that integrates methods and insights from multiple disciplines (such as psychology, sociology, law, and forensics) to understand and address criminal justice issues comprehensively.

6. APA Formatting

A set of standards for writing and documenting scholarly papers in the field of social sciences. Developed by the American Psychological Association, it specifies the organization, format, and citation guidelines for academic works.

7. Digital Literacy

The ability to effectively find, use, and communicate information in digital formats, including navigating online databases and utilizing digital tools for research and presentation in the context of criminal justice studies.

By understanding and applying these terms, you are laying the groundwork for success in your studies and your future career in criminal justice. Every term represents a stepping stone towards mastery in this dynamic field. As you progress, remember that these definitions are just the beginning. They invite you to delve deeper, ask questions, and seek out connections that will enrich your understanding and fortify your resolve to contribute to a just society.

References

1. Allen, D. (2001). Getting things done: The art of stress-free productivity. Penguin Books.

2. American Psychological Association. (2020). Publication manual of the American Psychological Association (7th ed.). https://www.apa.org

3. American Society of Criminology. (n.d.). About the ASC. Retrieved from https://asc41.com.

4. Arrigo, B. A. (2014). Ethics, Crime, and Criminal Justice (2nd ed.). Pearson.

5. Banks, C. (2016). Criminal Justice Ethics: Theory and Practice. Sage Publications.

6. Beccaria, C. (1764). On Crimes and Punishments.

7. Clear, T.R., Reisig, M.D., & Cole, G.F. (2020). American Corrections. Boston, MA: Cengage Learning.

8. Cole, G. F., Smith, C. E., & DeJong, C. (2019). The American system of criminal justice. Cengage Learning.

9. Davis, L. M., Steele, R. B., Williams, M. V., Turner, S., Miles, J. N. V., Saunders, J., & Steinberg, P. S. (2014). How effective is correctional education, and where do we go from here? The results of a comprehensive evaluation. Santa Monica, CA: RAND Corporation.

10. DioGuardi, S. (2016). Critical Thinking in Criminal Justice Ethics: Using the Affective Domain to Discover Gray Matters. Journal of Criminal Justice Education, 27(4), 535–548. https://doi.org/10.1080/10511253.2016.1145709

11. Ebbinghaus, H. (1885). Memory: A Contribution to Experimental Psychology. Dover Publications.

12. Flanagan, T. J. (2000). Liberal education and the criminal justice major. Journal of Criminal Justice Education, 11(1), 1–13. https://doi.org/10.1080/10511250000084721

13. Freeman, S., Eddy, S. L., McDonough, M., Smith, M. K., Okoroafor, N., Jordt, H., & Wenderoth, M. P. (2014). Active learning increases student performance in science, engineering, and mathematics. PNAS Proceedings of the National Academy of Sciences of the United States of America, 111(23), 8410–8415. https://doi.org/10.1073/pnas.1319030111

14. Graff, G., & Birkenstein, C. (2018). They say / I say: The moves that matter in academic writing (4th ed.). W. W. Norton & Company.

15. Jahromi, V. K., Tabatabaee, S. S., Abdar, ZE, & Rajabi M. Active listening: The key of successful communication in hospital managers. Electron Physician. 2016 Mar 25;8(3):2123-8. Doi: 10.19082/2123. PMID: 27123221; PMCID: PMC4844478.

16. Kolb, D. A. (1984). Experiential learning: Experience as the source of learning and development. Prentice-Hall.

17. Lee, C. (2017). How to write an APA style reference when information is missing. APA Style Blog. https://blog.apastyle.org/apastyle/reference-list/page/4/

18. Lipsey, M. W., Wilson, D. B., & Cothern, L. (2000). Effective intervention for serious juvenile offenders. Juvenile Justice Bulletin, Office of Justice Programs. Retrieved from https://www.ojp.gov/pdffiles1/ojjdp/181201.pdf

19. Locke, E. A., Shaw, K. N., Saari, L. M., & Latham, G. P. (1981). Goal setting and task performance: 1969–1980. Psychological Bulletin, 90(1), 125–152. https://doi.org/10.1037/0033-2909.90.1.125.

20. Lombroso, C. (1876). The Criminal Man.

21. MacKenzie, D. L. (2006). What works in corrections: Reducing the criminal activities of offenders and delinquents. Cambridge University Press.

22. Macan, T. H., Shahani, C., Dipboye, R. L., & Phillips, A. P. (1990). College students' time management: Correlations with academic performance and stress. Journal of Educational Psychology, 82(4), 760–768. https://doi.org/10.1037/0022-0663.82.4.760

23. Mendeley. (n.d.). Retrieved from https://www.mendeley.com/.

24. Merton, R. K. (1938). Social Structure and Anomie.

25. Miller, L. S., Hess, K. M., & Orthmann, C. H. (2014). Community policing: Partnerships for problem-solving. Cengage Learning.

26. Miller, L. S., Hess, K. M., & Orthmann, C. H. (2019). Community Policing: Partnerships for Problem Solving. Boston, MA: Cengage Learning.

27. Natarajan, M. (2011). International Crime and Justice. Cambridge University Press.

28. National Criminal Justice Association. (n.d.). Home. Retrieved from https://www.ncja.org.

29. National Criminal Justice Reference Service. (n.d.). Retrieved from https://www.ncjrs.gov/.

30. Neubauer, D. W., & Fradella, H. F. (2018). America's courts and the criminal justice system. Cengage Learning.

31. North, S. (1984). The Idea of a Writing Center. College English, 46(5), 433-446.

32. Pollock, J. M. (2013). Ethical Dilemmas and Decisions in Criminal Justice (8th ed.). Cengage Learning.

33. Purdue Online Writing Lab. (n.d.). APA Formatting and Style Guide. Retrieved from https://owl.purdue.edu/owl/research_and_citation/apa_style/apa_formatting_and_style_guide/general_format.html.

34. Purdue Online Writing Lab. (n.d.). APA formatting and style guide. https://owl.purdue.edu/owl/research_and_citation/apa_style/apa_formatting_and_style_guide/general_format.html

35. Reichel, P. L. (2008). Comparative Criminal Justice Systems: A Topical Approach. Prentice Hall.

36. Reichel, P. L. (2013). Comparative criminal justice systems: A topical approach. Pearson.

37. Rosenberg, G. N. (2008). The hollow hope: Can courts bring about social change? University of Chicago Press.

38. Shaw, C. R., & McKay, H. D. (1942). Juvenile Delinquency and Urban Areas.

39. Shelley, L. I. (2018). Dark Commerce: How a New Illicit Economy Is Threatening Our Future. Princeton University Press.

40. Shelley, L. I. (2018). Human trafficking: A global perspective. Cambridge University Press.

41. Stanton, T. K., Giles, D. E., & Cruz, N. I. (1999). Servicelearning: A movement's pioneers reflect on its origins, practice, and future. Jossey-Bass.

42. Stockdale, K. J., Sweeney, R., & McCluskey Dean, C. (2022). Exploring the Criminology Curriculum – Using the Intersectionality Matrix as a Pedagogical Tool to Develop Students' Critical Information Literacy Skills. Journal of

Criminal Justice Education, 33(4), 567–585. https://doi.org/10.1080/10511253.2021.2019290

43. Sweitzer, H. F., & King, M. A. (2009). The successful internship: Personal, professional, and civic development in experiential learning. Brooks/Cole.

44. Walker, S., & Katz, C. M. (2018). The Police in America: An introduction. McGraw-Hill Education.

45. Zehr, H. (2002). The little book of restorative justice: Revised and updated. Good Books.

46. Zimmerman, B. J., & Kitsantas, A. (2002). Acquiring writing revision and self-regulatory skill through observation and emulation. Journal of Educational Psychology, 94(4), 660–668. https://doi.org/10.1037/0022-0663.94.4.660

47. Zims, J. E., Weissberg, R. P., Wang, M. C., & Walberg, H. J. (2004). Building Academic Success on Social and Emotional Learning: What Does the Research Say? New York City, New York; Teachers College Press.

48. Zotero. (n.d.). Retrieved from https://www.zotero.org/

www.ingramcontent.com/pod-product-compliance
Lightning Source LLC
LaVergne TN
LVHW022110200926
848481LV00003B/1132
9798385144280